D0162430

MIRRORS AND MASKS:
THE SEARCH FOR IDENTITY

MIRRORS
AND MASKS

The Search for Identity

BY ANSELM L. STRAUSS

UNIVERSITY OF CALIFORNIA MEDICAL CENTER
SAN FRANCISCO, CALIFORNIA

THE SOCIOLOGY PRESS

TO MY WIFE, FRANCES

Contents

Preface

IDENTITY as a concept is fully as elusive as is everyone's sense of his own personal identity. But whatever else it may be, identity is connected with the fateful appraisals made of oneself—by oneself and by others. Everyone presents himself to the others and to himself, and sees himself in the mirrors of their judgments. The masks he then and thereafter presents to the world and its citizens are fashioned upon his anticipations of their judgments. The others present themselves too; they wear their own brands of mask and they get appraised in turn. It is all a little like the experience of the small boy first seeing himself (at rest and posing) in the multiple mirrors at the barber shop or in the tailor's triple mirrors.

Identity is not a new word, any more than is ego or self; and like these latter terms its referents are, as Erik Erikson[1] has pointed out, admittedly vague. But the notion of identity has served me, as it so brilliantly served him, as an agent for organizing materials and thoughts about certain aspects of problems traditionally intriguing to social psychologists. (I shall name the problems in a moment.) In thinking about those problems I experienced, as perhaps does everyone, a kind of partial paralysis that seizes one when he operates with conventional concepts (such as role and status and reference group). By deliberately choosing an ambiguous, diffuse term like identity I sensed that I could better look around the corners of my problems, and be less likely to slide down the well-worn grooves of other men's thought.

Now as to the problems: social psychologists have long been engaged in thinking about, and studying, such matters as group membership, motivation, personality development and social interaction. Because we all have, in a certain sense, dual allegiance and training, it is too much to expect that these problems will provoke the same kinds of inquiries by all. Although social psychologists talk each others' language —at least in some sense—we also equally and legitimately think like anthropologists, psychologists, psychiatrists and sociologists; with an eye on the main theoretical interests of the discipline in which we were chiefly trained. We are oriented not only toward other social psychologists but toward colleagues in our "own" fields—and sometimes rather more toward the latter. Even when we use the same concepts and express an interest in the same problems, it usually turns out that we employ the concepts dissimilarly and pose far from identical questions in our research. But I do not wish to overstate either the impermeability of boundaries nor their immutability: my intention is to set the stage for maintaining that even the long-standing problems of social psychology will, and should, provoke different kinds of inquiry from men who have inherited, or created, different perspectives—and I wish to outline my own against this contrasting background.

I began by trying to think through some of the implications of the symbolic interaction approach—a point of view stemming from the pragmatists and from the work of several earlier sociologists—which stresses the crucial role of language for human behavior. It also stresses a kind of openended, partially unpredictable, view of events: interaction is regarded as guided by rules, norms, mandates; but its outcomes are assumed to be not always, or entirely, determinable in advance. This indeterminacy need not be a stumbling block to scientific research, but has to be taken into account.

At the same time, I had been dissatisfied with much of the theory and research about self, ego and personality, because in this work the influence of social organization is so greatly underestimated, its role so insufficiently understood. Social psychology, it seemed to me, should have much to offer its sister fields, but only insofar as its practitioners can self-consciously tie their work back to the social organizational heart of sociology and anthropology. In sum: my essay ought properly to be regarded as an attempt to juxtapose and fuse symbolic interactional and social organizational perspectives into a workable, suggestive social psychology.

As I began to write, I found myself drawn into using the essay form. Nowadays there is a relatively undisguised bias against theoretical essays, except when they are short or are speeches. But the essay is too nice a form to be so easily abandoned. In a peculiar way it frees both the author and the reader by its very tone and style of attack upon problems. This does not make it any less a vehicle of thought, although the ideas do not necessarily march across its pages in clearly marshalled, or in propositional, order. If I have taken the long way around stylistically speaking—drawing upon the connotative impact of language as well as upon its more denotative resources—my strategy has been purposive.

The essay is divided into six chapters, each building upon the preceding. In the first chapter, I begin to spell out the basic importance of language for human action and identity. I stress "naming" as an act of placement or classification—of self and others. Implicit in such placements is the evaluation of persons and their acts. The chapter closes with a discussion of rhetoric, or the legitimate and understandable quarrels over "proper" classification that mark human concourse.

In chapter two, I stress the perpetual indeterminancy of identities in constantly changing social contexts. The intent of this chapter is to lay groundwork for a later and more detailed discussion of identity change, for interaction, and for what it means to be a "member" of a group. Some familiar problems of self and self-appraisal are touched upon. To them is added a consideration of such matters as commitment, possession, alienation and sacrifice.

Chapter three turns about the symbolic and developmental character of human interaction. I take the stand that sociological preoccupation with group structure requires a more detailed analysis of interaction than yet exists—although a number of scholars are moving in this direction—and that the invention of that analysis will be mutually useful for studying groups and members of groups. I begin with an attempt to make explicit a view of motivation that is implicit in many sociological research reports; then stress the complexity and fluid character of interaction. The bulk of the discussion in this chapter consists of suggestions for viewing and analyzing interaction along lines consistent with my interests in problems of social organization.

In chapter four, I take up the theme of identity—changes in ways quite familiar to students of anthropology and sociology, using much of their vocabulary. I attempt mainly to spell out implications in this body of research for changes in adult behavior and identity—dealing mainly with patterned changes, both those institutionally controlled and those consequential upon it but escaping it.

Chapter five can be thought of as an extension of the preceding one. I examine first some relations between generations, and suggest that these relations need to be taken much more into account than is done in current writing about personality development. This discussion is followed by some speculations concerning how changes of identity are minimized; and how, despite such change, persons experience a sense of oneness or continuity.

In the last chapter, the symbolic character of membership in groups is made explicit—a matter that has in preceding pages been left implicit. I am led to look at membership in less "structural" ways than is commonly done, and to take the position that students of identity should think in historical, as well as autobiographical, terms. If taken seriously, this implies different (or at least supplementary) training from that which is usual among social psychologists and sociologists. At the end of the essay, there is appended a short concluding note.

Some readers may wonder why I have nowhere defined "identity." This is related to my decision not to deal with a problem with which both psychologists and psychiatrists are centrally concerned—namely the structure, or organization, of personality. One reason is that sociological and anthropological writing is not particularly rich in theory or research about this area (aside from specifying various social conditions under which types of personalities are produced and flourish). Some readers of this essay may be disappointed, reasoning that something purporting to be about identity ought to deal with its organization. But mainly I am suggesting ways of theorizing about, and doing research upon, the social processes from which identity emerges (at least in part): about the symbolic and cultural foundations of its structure. And again, as Kai Erikson has suggested to me, I am discussing a facet of identity: that aspect of my subject which deals not with "ego identity" but with how persons become implicated with other persons and are affected, and affect each other, through that implication.

It is my hope that psychiatrists and psychologists, although they will surely miss the stress upon ego-identity, will profit from my emphasis upon social organization and language. I would be disappointed if sociologists did not, in turn, find useful my attempt to pull social psychology and social organization together. Sociologists, as I say in the last pages of the essay, have either to invent their own brand of social psychology or borrow it from neighboring fields. They usually do the former (although there might be some contention about that). I take it that it is better to be explicit than implicit, better to work out a social psychology than to borrow it.

In the writing of this book, I owe much to probing questions raised during seminars at the University of Chicago during the years 1952 to 1956, and to students whose theses in part utilized ideas expressed in the original hectographed manuscript of four years ago. I am especially indebted for verbal exchange of ideas and reading of manuscript to Howard Becker, of Community Studies, Incorporated of Kansas City; to Nelson Foote, of the General Electric Corporation; Erving Goffman, of the University of California; Donald Horton of the Bank Street School of Education, New York City; Orrin Klapp, of the University of San Diego; David Riesman, of Harvard University; Melvin Sabshin, of the Psychosomatic and Psychiatric Institute at Michael Reese Hospital in Chicago; Leonard Schatzman, of the Psychosomatic and Psychiatric Institute at Michael Reese Hospital; W. Lloyd Warner, of the University of Chicago; and to my late colleague, R. Richard Wohl. I am grateful, too, for helpful commentary on the manuscript to Herbert Blumer, of the University of California; Kai Erikson, of the University of Pittsburgh; Blanche Geer, of Community Studies, Incorporated; Gregory Stone, of the University of Missouri; and to G. E. Swanson, of the University of Michigan; also to E. C. Hughes of the University of Chicago, and to A. R. Lindesmith of Indiana University. I am especially grateful to my former colleague, Nelson Foote, because it was he who initiated a group project which provided the incentive for writing this essay.

CHAPTER ONE

Language and Identity

CENTRAL to any discussion of identity is language. The word "central" is used advisedly. Language is ofttimes construed as just one more kind of behavior—encompassing speaking, reading, writing, and hearing—within a long listing of other kinds of behavior. An important and recurring theme of this essay is that a proper theoretical account of men's identities and action must put men's linguistics into the heart of the discussion.

Names

Consider, as a beginning, that *distinctive appelation by which a person is known*: his name. A name can be very revealing, both of its donor and its owner; if we are observant we shall find it speaks volumes. First generation Jewish immigrants to this country were called by old-fashioned names resounding with rich historical overtones, names like Isaac, Benjamin, Abraham, Hannah, and Ruth; but the children of their children are hardly ever named after such Biblical models, since as their styles of life change, so have their ideals and aspirations. The children's names represent this change if not as precisely, at least as surely, as pink litmus signifies acid. Any name is a container; poured into it are the conscious or unwitting evaluations of the namer. Sometimes this is obvious, as when post-civil war Negroes named their children after the Great Emancipator; sometimes the position of the namer has to be sought and one's inference buttressed by other evidence.

If the name reveals the judgments of the namer, what of the person who receives it? How does he react to this attempt to fix his identity in some way, beforehand? There is a range here running from relative indifference to violent rejection or prideful acceptance. There is the name that announces its bearer to be the third of a line of famous personages, destined not to be the last to do it honor. Probably more common in this country are those names over which children have blushed and been ashamed as their teachers stuttered over pronunciation, these names often later to be shortened, discarded, or relegated to alphabetized shorthand. The point is not whether or not a man can be wholly indifferent to his name but that an extensive range of reaction can be evoked by his imaginings of what he must look like to certain audiences if he bears the name that he does.

The names that are adopted voluntarily reveal even more tellingly the indissoluble tie between name and self-image. The changing of names marks a rite of passage. It means such things as that the person wants to have the kind of name he thinks represents him as a person, does not want any longer to be the kind of person that his previous name signified. The commonest and perhaps least emotionally charged instance of name-changing occurs when a bride takes over her husband's last name and so signifies her changed status. Suppose the wife of an American male were to insist that he change his last name to hers! The phenomenon of "passing" is often marked by name-changing: you disguise who you were or are in order to appear what you wish to be. Benny Ginsburgh may become Basil Gainsborough to express—not necessarily passing and secrecy—but only mobility aspirations. Secrecy sometimes gets mingled with personality transition, as when revolutionists adopt new names and thus seek to bury publicly their pasts; but the new names also mark passage to new self-images. Conversion, religious or otherwise, is often marked by a complete change of name, that act signifying the person's new status in the eyes of God, the world, and himself—marking status and setting a seal upon it.

Less complete changes of status are commonly marked by the partial qualifications of name through the addition of a title, as if to say "this man is now a member of the Senate, so let us accord him his due and address him as Senator." There are some names, like titles, that have to be earned; having earned them, one tells himself that this is what he is and that other people think so too or they would not so address him. Some Indian tribes, for instance, recognized a warrior's major achievement in battle by sanctioning an entire change of name. Americans use a similar device in applying nicknames to express earned status, and by them, can denote a change in status.

Names have to do also with "qualities" and "classifications." This is illustrated in a haunting speech in the Carson McCullers play "Member of the Wedding." Frankie, a lonely twelve year old girl, in search of an elusive and formative self-picture, is speaking in fantasy to the Negro maid, Berenice, about her relations with a brother and his bride-to-be.[1]

> FRANKIE: Janice and Jarvis. It gives me this pain just to think about them.
> BERENICE: It is a known truth that gray-eyed people are jealous.
> FRANKIE: I told you I wasn't jealous. I couldn't be jealous of one of them without being jealous of them both. I 'sociate the two of them together. Somehow they're just so different from us. . . . J.A.—Janice and Jarvis. Isn't that the strangest thing?
> BERENICE: What?

FRANKIE: J. A.—Both their names begin with "J. A."

BERENICE: And? What about it?

FRANKIE: If only my name was Jane. Jane or Jasmine.

BERENICE: I don't follow your frame of mind.

FRANKIE: Jarvis and Janice and Jasmine. See?

BERENICE: No. I don't see.

FRANKIE: I wonder if it's against the law to change your name. Or add to it.

BERENICE: Naturally. It's against the law.

FRANKIE (*impetuously*): Well, I don't care. F. Jasmine Addams.

In one swift moment of revelation she has moved another step toward discovering who and what she is, and with whom and in what sense she belongs. "J" marks the boundary not simply of three persons, but is a circle drawn snugly around a class of identical persons and their identical attributes. "J" stands for F. Jasmine's essential being or substance, at least for the moment, and has to do with belonging to the class of J's whose attributes are those suggested in the fantasy itself and are opposed to those of all other people who, *pari passu*, are classed as non-J's. The child-like quality of F. Jasmine's speech should not blind us to the fact that a naming of self is always a genuine placement or categorization. This can be more clearly perceived if the scope of this discussion is widened to include naming as an act.

Naming as an Act of Placement

The philosophers, John Dewey and Arthur Bentley, in *Knowing and the Known*, have argued that to name is to know, and that the extent of knowing is dependent upon the extent of the naming. By this they do not mean to suggest anything magical about the act of naming, but to make that act central to any human's cognition of his world. This view informs much of the discussion that will follow.

Suppose a mother wishes her very young child to pay attention to an object. She moves his body so that his eyes focus somewhere near the object and then she points toward it. But when he is at an age when he can respond to a word, she will hope to attract his attention more efficiently to some thing by naming it. This is what is called "ostensive definition," meaning an indication of an object without any description whatever; it is the simplest kind of identification. The first identifications are singular; they indicate particular objects. But the child soon learns that certain objects can be called by the same word, albeit his groupings are frequently amusing and seem incorrect to his elders. At first parents often bow to the child's peculiar classification of objects, in order to keep peace in the family, but in the end they win the game, for the youngster must eventually conform to more conventional, if less colorful, lexicology.

To name, then, is not only to indicate; it is to identify an object as some kind of object. An act of identification requires that the thing referred to be placed within a category. Borrowing from the language of logic, we may say that any particular object that is referred to is a member of a general class, a representative of that class. An orange is a member of a class called oranges; but note that this class itself receives its placement, or definition, only by virtue of its relationships with other classes. These relationships are of quite a systematic sort. Thus oranges may be defined in relation to such classes as fruits, foods, tropical growths, tree products, and moderately priced objects. Defining any class, then, means relating it to systematically associated classes. "To tell what a thing is, you place it in terms of something else. This idea of locating, or placing, is implicit in our very word for definition itself: to *define*, or *determine* a thing, is to mark its boundaries."[2]

It should be noted, however, that any particular object can be named, and thus located, in countless ways. The naming sets it within a context of quite differently related classes. The nature or essence of an object does not reside mysteriously within the object itself but is dependent upon how it is defined by the namer. An object which looks so much like an orange—in fact which really is an orange—can also be a member of an infinite number of other classes. If it is in its nature to be an orange, it is also in its nature to be other things. In the case of an orange, we may choose to view it within different contexts for other equally legitimate purposes. It may thus be viewed as a spherical object, with rough, warm-colored skin, suitable for catching and casting lights, hence eminently definable as a model for a beginning art student. Essentially it is just that. This is only to repeat a point made earlier that to name or designate is always to do this from some point of view. From a single identical perspective otherwise seemingly different things can be classed together. Justification lies in the perspective, not in the things. If you do not agree with your neighbor's classification, this may only signify that you have a somewhat or wholly different basis for drawing symbolic circles around things.

The way in which things are classed together reveals, graphically as well as symbolically, the perspectives of the classifier. For instance, an anthropologist (Robert Pehrson) studying the Laplanders recently discovered that a single word is used to encompass both "people" and "reindeer." The life of the Laplander revolves around activities having to do with reindeer. Is a reindeer a human or is a human a reindeer? The question is senseless; the people and reindeer are identified, they go together, and the very fact of their identification in terminology gives the anthropologist one of his best clues to the Laplanders' ordering of the world and its objects.

Any group of people that has any permanence develops a "special language," a lingo or jargon, which represents its way of identifying those objects important for group action. Waitresses classify types of customers and other workers in the restaurant, give shorthand names to foods, and have special signs and gestures standing for important activities. So do criminals; and even ministers are not immune from the necessity of classifying their clientele and colleagues, otherwise how could they organize activity in an orderly and sensible manner?

The propensity for certain categories invented by any group to be slanderous, to partake of epithet, derogation and innuendo, has been bemoaned by liberals, debunkers, teachers, and all others who have wished to set other's classifications straight. Since groups inevitably are in conflict over issues—otherwise they would not be different groups—and since events inevitably come to be viewed differently by those who are looking up or down opposite ends of the gun, it is useless to talk of trying to eradicate from the human mind the tendency to stereotype, to designate nastily, and to oversimplify. This is not to say that humans are brutish, but that they are thoroughly human. Animals do not name-call, neither do they possess or assign identities in the elaborate sense in which we are discussing identity.

Classification and the Direction of Action

This necessity for any group to develop a common or shared terminology leads to an important consideration: the direction of activity depends upon the particular ways that objects are classified. This can be simply illustrated. Not so long ago, children used to be fed large quantities of spinach according to the syllogism that spinach contained iron and that iron was needed for building bones. Now it appears that excessive consumption of spinach reduces body calcium and therefore is bad for the bones. Spinach is thus reclassified and only if you wish to reduce calcium content should you overindulge. The renaming of any object, then, amounts to a reassessment of your relation to it, and *ipso facto* your behavior becomes changed along the line of your reassessment. In any event it is the definition of what the object "is" that allows action to occur with reference to what it is taken to be. Mark Twain tells how as an apprentice pilot he mistook a wind reef (not dangerous) for a bluff reef (deadly dangerous) and, to the hilarity of his boss who "properly" read the signs, performed miraculous feats of foolishness to avoid the murderous pseudo-bluff.

The naming of an object provides a directive for action, as if the object were forthrightly to announce, "You say I am this, then act in the appropriate way toward me." Conversely, if the actor feels he does not know what the object is, then with regard to it his action is blocked. Suppose that in the dark one reached for a glass of milk, raised it to his lips, recoiled at the strange taste, and stood immobilized until he was able to label the taste as tomato juice. Energy for action was there, but was temporarily unharnessed, immobilized, until naming occurred. Of course, in this example the moment of immobilization would be fleeting, since as soon as one set about to discover what the taste was he would be acting toward something belonging to the category of "unidentified liquid, whose nature is to be discovered." A person need not be certain that he knows what an object is in order to organize a line of action toward it—he merely has to be willing to take a chance on his judgment.

Classification and Evaluation

An act of classification not only directs overt action, but arouses a set of expectations toward the object thus classified. A chair ought to hold anyone who sits on it, not turn into a piano or a cat, and a buzzing housefly should not piteously ask us not to swat her, saying she is a fairy in disguise. We are surprised only if our expectations are unfulfilled, as when a presumed salesman in a department store assures us that he is just an ordinary shopper like ourselves, or when milk turns out to be strongly spiked with rum. When we classify, our expectations necessarily face both past and future. Expectations have to do with consequential relations between ourselves and the object. However expectations rest also upon remembrances of past experiences with objects resembling— we believe—the one currently before us.

Since this is so, classifications not only carry our anticipations but also those values that were experienced when we encountered the things, persons, or events now classified. For example, the Japanese have a food called "tofu" which is a soy-bean product. Let us imagine that the first time we meet tofu it is served cold with soy sauce over it and that it strikes us as unpalatable. Tofu is for us an indifferent food, and if at some future time we should see tofu or hear the word our images would likely be of the indifferent experience we had with a whitish jellied object covered with brown sauce. But suppose that some time later we are treated to a delicious soup in which there are pieces of a mushy substance. "What is that good stuff in the soup?" we ask, and are surprised to find it is cooked tofu. Now we revise our evaluation: tofu in soup, good; tofu uncooked, not so good. This substance, as used by the Japanese, appears in several guises, so yet more surprises may be in store for us. The range of our experience with tofu is both what we know of it and how we value it. The wider grows this range, the better we know the object—what it can do and what can be done with it—and likewise the more extensive become our judgments of its capacities and qualities. It would appear that classification, knowledge and value are inseparable.

There are several more lessons suggested by the illustration. One is that values attributed to any object—like "good" or "hateful"—really are not "in" the object. In having an experience one does not put value into it like water into a kettle. Value is not an element; it has to do with a relation between the object and the person who has experiences with the object. This is just another way of stating that the "essence" or "nature" of the object resides not in the object but in the relation between it and the namer. Value as a relation is easily seen in conjunction with such an adjective as "useful"—useful for whom, under what conditions, for which of his purposes? Precisely the same is true whether the object is a thing or an event, and whether the value is "useful" or, say, "sinful." Sinfulness is not fixed in the event, a quality of it within the eye of God. An act is sinful to particular definers when perceived as committed under certain circumstances by persons of specified identities.

Since values are not in objects but are evaluations of objects, it follows that persons must do their own experiencing in order to do their own evaluating. This does not mean that I cannot teach you the meaning of something prior to your direct experience of it. I can say that the dust rises off the city streets in a certain country and constantly hangs so heavy in the air that it is hard to breath. You have experienced similar conditions, so readily understand. But when you are introduced to a new terminology, the best you can do is draw upon possibly analogous experiences, and these may or may not lead to accurate conceptions. To experience, hence to evaluate, a Balinese trance as do the Balinese probably cannot even be approximated by an American. Everyone has at some time been introduced to new terms representing new ways of looking at objects, as when entering upon a new job. Such occupational terms cannot be fully grasped, the objects and events be perceived as others perceive them, until we have undergone similar experiences ourselves. Of course an articulate informant drawing colorfully and accurately upon whatever is similar in his and your experiences can bring you to closer comprehension and appreciation; hence the great usefulness of some novels and biographies. But no amount of description in advance, if the shift in perspective called for is radical, will teach you how you yourself will finally evaluate. You yourself must do, suffer, and undergo —to use John Dewey's terms.[3]

As people "undergo," their evaluations change. Values are not eternal. Expectations cannot always be fulfilled. Things change; so do we. "Good things change and vanish not only with changes in the environing medium but with changes in ourselves."[4] Even without direct new experience something novel may be learned about an object—such as one might learn something new about life in prison, or as when a college student studies about geological strata and rainfall and so comes into somewhat different relationships with rocks, rain, and water. As long as learning continues, revision of concepts continues; and as long as revision takes place, reorganization of behavior takes place.

The naming or identifying of things is, then, a continual problem, never really over and done with. By continual I do not mean continuous—one can lie in a hammock contentedly watching the moon rise and raising no questions about it, the world, or oneself. Nevertheless, some portion of one's classificatory terminology, the symbolic screen through which the world is ordered and organized, is constantly under strain—or just has been—or will be. George H. Mead (who asserted that classifications are really hypotheses) would say it necessarily must be, from the very nature of action which brings in its train the reconstruction of past experience and the arising of new objects.[5]

Rhetoric as a Terminological Debate

It is precisely this continual necessity for reassessment that permits the innovation and novelty of human life. If expectations were always fulfilled—if present situations and events were exactly as anticipated from experiences with past ones—then action would be thoroughly ritualistic, and conceptions eternally static. Innovation, in fact, rests upon ambiguous, confused, not wholly defined situations. Out of ambiguity arises challenge and the discovery of new values: "it is in the areas of ambiguity that transformations take place . . . without such areas transformation would be impossible."[6]

Emergent valuation is hardly a serene process, for the reassessment of experience is apt to be quite stressful. When some object or event is pinned down so that you think you know what it is, then you have the illusion that this portion at least, of your world is known. But let the object step out of character and it becomes quickly apparent that whatever it was, it no longer is. There is even the possibility that it was never what you thought it to be. Then what is it, how are you to assess it, define it, act toward it, and for what purposes; and what are you, yourself, in relation to it?

Since classification and evaluation are not merely private acts but are usually, if not predominantly, public concerns, problematic situations and issues are foci of public contention as well as private debate. At the very minimum two perspectives will appear. One of these may be represented by an old guard which maintains that the situation has not really changed at all. When changes are admitted by this latter group, they may be explained away as not "substantially" or "essentially" altering the main character of the object or event; for instance, it is maintained that some changes have occurred in the federal government during and since the war, but that it remains essentially the same type of government. Precisely these changes will be seized upon by opponents who argue that the new characteristics are substantial enough to warrant new definition. Contention for terminological prizes is not mere squabbling over words, for words are mandates for action, and sometimes classificatory decision involves a matter of life and death. At the very least, men's interests are deeply involved.

An example of a jurisdictional battle may be of use here. In institutions, such as hospitals, different groups contend over who has the proper right to do certain things and who has not. Is this act to be a nurse's act or an attendant's act? Is it the job of a doctor to reprimand the medical technician, or does the right belong only to the technician's boss? Such disputes may be settled by higher authorities who may define the act formally, but of course in reality the argument and rule-breaking may continue. In relatively stabilized areas of behavior, jurisdictions are fairly clear and challenge is absent. But the emergence of new occupational groups necessarily results in jurisdictional struggle, for old and new groups see their interests being whittled away or closed off. As legal and occupational rights are fought over and compromised, the fate of the occupational group emerges. The meaning of being a doctor or an osteopath or a nurse, or anything else, is a thoroughly temporal matter.

Cynicism and bitterness are likely to hang heavy over the rhetorical battleground. Strife lends itself to the conviction that one's opponents are arguing wholly from motives of self-interest. As Kenneth Burke has remarked, "rhetoric is par excellence the region of the Scramble, of insult and injury, bickering, squabbling, malice, and the lie, cloaked malice and the subsidized lie."[7] The unctuous radio announcer reeling off the marvelous qualities of his sponsor's product is a classical target for skeptics; and propaganda as a word, if not as a fact, has become suspect. The assumption

that supports any discounting of opponents' arguments is
that the situation is what it is, and the opponents know
what it is but they deny or obscure this fact with clear consciousness. If malevolence or self-interest seem improbable,
then blindness or stupidity can be held accountable for the
muddying of waters. Think of any hotly debated current
public issue and you will have this point illustrated.

True, there is enough calculation of audience-reaction to
make it obvious that a fair amount of verbal manipulation
does occur. Hence debunking, motive-mongering, and ex-
posés have some point. But there is a much more fundamental
point at issue here, revolving around the question of what
happens when people of good intentions but divergent perspectives cannot agree. Fortunate indeed is the game that
has an umpire, but most games are for keeps and judgments
will not easily be ceded to higher authority. It comes down
to this: both sides will make out the best case they can for
the way they view matters, and the audience or audiences
can choose one or the other or neither.

Although many strategies, tactics, and techniques are used
in the debate, it is its terminological aspect that I wish to
stress. The attempt to make an argument for a position can
be imagined as a game whereby circles are drawn which en-
close different terrain than circles drawn by an opponent. A
professor of statistics at a large university once gave a speech
to his colleagues in which he argued that no faculty member
should speak to a public audience except on his own subject
and about matters upon which there was unequivocal expert
concensus. Rhetorically speaking, how is the speaker classifying things? Professors are experts, otherwise presumably they
would not be hired to teach their specialties. There are
classes of experts: some are inside and some outside the university. Professors are university members and have obligations pertaining to this status. A university is many kinds of
"thing," but substantially it stands in relation to the wider

public as teacher—"teacher" meaning transmitter of verified knowledge. A different kind of teaching can occur within the university where a different kind of student than the public is found: one who is critical, capable of handling a hypothetical argument and recognizing one when he sees it. Although the professor is a citizen, he is a certain kind of citizen; his verbal and public contribution to the commonwealth is through his role of expert. In answer to his argument, innumerable other ways of drawing circumferences are possible. Are professors essentially professors, or essentially citizens whose first duties are to contribute to the public clarification of important issues? Is the university essentially a repository and transmitter of verified knowledge or something else, for instance the stimulator of profound controversy? The classifications cross and crisscross and "the wavering line between . . . cannot be 'scientifically' identified; rival rhetoricians can draw it at different places."[8]

All this is reflected in individual experience for, as members of groups, persons internalize the rhetorical battles. Situations arise that are not easily placed into comfortable rubrics—when dilemmas are posed and stands must be taken. If the inner dialogue concerns matters felt to be important by the person, then turmoil marks his progress, either toward choice of that horn of the dilemma finally seized or towards the novel decision that bridges the dilemma. A genuine outsider can only marvel at the blindness of the person for limiting the battle to this particular terrain, or wonder why there was a battle at all. But one who shares his concepts can empathize and understand, though not necessarily agree with his decision. Because he is limited to participating in a relatively small number of groups, his conceptions of imagined consummations or values are limited also. The possibility of alteration in anyone's range of vision is increased by intimate participation in groups composed of people as unlike oneself as possible. If one associates only

with his counterparts there is less chance for radical conceptual change, despite the inevitable splintering and dissidence
into sub-groupings, for rivals may really be much alike. In
any event, the alternative paths of action staked out during
the battle for proper vision are limited by the person's terminologies: those that enter into the battle and those that
develop as a consequence of it.

Language, it should now be abundantly clear, is far from
peripheral to the study of human action and identity. This
chapter opened with a statement to this effect, and the entire
essay will be seen to represent a working out of implications
flowing from this basic position. Some of the implications
drawn will appear quite correct, others more remote. I shall
show first some of the more obvious ones, turning now to
how people act in ways sometimes surprising to themselves,
and the consequent re-evaluations of self that this occasions.
Re-evaluation, however intermittent, points to the unfinished, never-ending quality of each individual life; and this
raises theoretical considerations centering around the attainment and loss of self-possession, of commitment to values. My
discussion is pointed, by implication, against too ready an assumption of engrained and early formed character-structure.
It also asserts a position (which I shall elaborate later, since
here the position is presented only obliquely) that continuities of personal experience are systematically related to
those provided by social structure, but are not assured by
social structure. I wish, too, to underscore the creative possibilities, as well as the hazardous, of discontinuity.

CHAPTER TWO

Self-Appraisals
and the Course of Action

Interdeterminancy and the Self

TO SAY that men use language is to say that they must evaluate the past, the present, and the future. Regardless of how any society's vocabulary may cut and order temporal flow, past and future impinge upon and influence action in the present. The human experience of time is one of process: the present is always a "becoming"; it is always coming up, as the future moves toward us, or it is moving away as present action recedes into the past. The peculiarly elusive quality of present experience often has been commented upon, for although we can be perfectly aware of present action, we can pass judgment upon it only when it is already a moment past: "I cannot turn around quickly enough to catch myself."[1] An action can be evaluated immediately after its performance—so immediately that it feels subjectively as if evaluation and action occurred simultaneously. However, G. Ryle reminds us that "my commentary on my performances must always be silent about one performance, and this performance can be the target only of another commentary."[2] During a sequence of action I may guide and change my course by making evaluations of immediately past actions. When the sequence, or entire act, is finished, I may of course sum up what transpired and how it turned out.

The evaluation of recent performances is frequently neces-
sitated by the fact that they surprise even the actor himself.
The surprising quality of the act, of course, has limits; an
outfielder may be astonished by the ball slipping out of his
hand or by an exceptionally accurate throw to home plate;
but he does not astonish himself by stopping to caress the
ball before throwing it. In the very nature of having to
handle objects which may be yielding or recalcitrant to one's
purposes, men make fools of themselves, or heroes, without
intention. There are perhaps other reasons for unexpected
outcomes. Ryle suggests that in anticipating future action,
the "process of pre-envisaging may divert the course of my
ensuing behavior in a direction and degree of which my
prognosis cannot take account."[3] Last moment cues also may
divert or redirect action, as well as happenings during the
course of the action, providing it has duration at all. Psychiatrists would suggest responses to cues in the situation whose
presence was not consciously formulated by the actor. Whatever the explanation, the unexpected does occur to our
varying astonishment, anguish, chagrin, and delight.

An act performed is, in a certain sense, never finished,
unless it becomes quite forgotten. Most acts, of course, are
forgotten, but the very possibility of recollection permits
re-evaluation. This may be thoroughly unwitting, for implicit
in the process of recollecting is selectivity and a reconstruction of the actual happening; certain aspects of the remembered action drop out or are slighted, others are highlighted.
We do not necessarily change our minds about past acts,
but we may; some acts, deemed important, may be reassessed
many times over, as one gets new orientations or new facts.

This propensity for humans to judge their own acts has
led various writers to speak of the self making itself its own
object. A person who is judging anyone's act is doing so as
a "subject." The act or person being judged is an "object."
Any man can be both, simultaneously; having acted, he may

make his act an object of scrutiny. He may take as many different stances toward it as his vocabulary permits, just as he may toward another's. His own act may be his object of scorn, denial, discount, blame, attack, shame, disapproval, a yardstick for further endeavors, a cross to bear, a sign of personal brilliance, or anything else that he has the capacity to view it as. And if he should acquire new terminology through new group participations, he will inevitably reassess certain of his past acts—and himself—in the new terms. The self is no more immune to re-examination from new perspectives than any other object.

The complexity of actions toward other persons is matched by actions toward self. I have already touched upon the range and variety of evaluative operations, but the object of evaluation has complex aspects also. This is suggested by a philosopher's statement (Kurt Riezler) that, "The Me can mean many things; the Me of yesterday, today, or tomorrow, or the Me of everyday, the Me in this particular action or situation, or the Me in all actions or situations."[4] Questions can be raised by me concerning my previous judgments— whether of particular acts, of long sequences of action, of the propriety of gesture or emotional display, of things said and how they are said; questions may even be raised about the "essential self," the self that I believe to be behind or underneath all my acts.

The reappraisal of past acts and the appearance of surprise in present acts gives men indeterminate futures. Thus, in appraising the meaning of the unexpected, new value and worth are found. Values are consummated and—now formulated—become targets for reattainment; they will be striven for under similar or different conditions. Also, although values consummated in the past now provide ends for actions, the reassessment of current acts means that courses get changed, paths abandoned. Self-appraisal leads to decisions: to avoid acts, to make amends, to do better, to repent, to do as well. Self-appraisal is thus "surrounded by a halo of 'can' and 'cannot,' 'will' and 'will not,' 'should' and 'should not.' "[5] The I, as subject, in reviewing its Me's as objects, continually moves into a partially uncharted future; thus new I's and Me's—that is, appraising acts and appraised acts—necessarily emerge.

All this is equally true of groups that have histories. The temporal spans of group life mean that the aims and aspirations of group endeavor are subject to review and recasting. Likewise past activities come to be viewed in new lights, through reappraisal and selective recollection. It would be an unjustifiable reification to say that the group becomes an object to itself, but it is perfectly reasonable to declare that, through communicative processes, the group members develop shared judgments about both the future and past meanings of their affiliations. History, whether that of a single person or of a group, signifies a "coming back at self"[6] —a matter I shall return to in some detail near the close of this essay.

Although I have thus far focused upon the actor irrespective of other actors, it is obvious that in self-appraisal the responses of others must be taken into account. In anticipating what your act is going to look like to those others who will in turn respond to it, you see your future act as in a kind of complicated mirror.

> *Each to each a looking-glass*
> *Reflects the other that doth pass.*[7]

The audiences that will respond may be on the scene or far away; they may be specific other persons, or they may be so generalized as to be the equivalent of "they" or "the Gods"; and they may be alive or long dead ("what would she have said?") or as yet unborn ("what will they say?"). Whether an act is ritualistic or problematic, such anticipations of others' responses enter into its organization.

The mirror image, of course, can be grossly inaccurate; the consequences can be quite different than foreseen. Sometimes consequences can be discounted, explained away, as merely complicated and perverse instances of what was expected. (Because this is especially characteristic of the reactions of some types of psychotics, the psychiatrist, H. S. Sullivan, adopted the therapeutic strategy of crossing his schizophrenic patients' expectations at dramatically critical points.) Frequently, the responses of others are bound to appear out of tune with our expectations. This impels the re-evaluation of acts, for other persons often express in unequivocal terms just what they think of our actions. If they do not express forthright judgment, then the meaning of their responses sometimes must be ferreted out. Our judgments are made atop their judgments. Shall we agree, disagree, how much and in what sense?

I have already, when discussing rhetoric, noted that as novel situations and unfamiliar acts are met, extensions of vocabulary are called for. These new terms must be justified to significant other persons, who may be skeptical of our conceptual solutions. This process of ratification or validation —to use a legal terminology—is important for various reasons, chief among them that certain other persons must be brought to organize acts in like terminology; otherwise they and we cannot participate together in shared activity. But there are, of course, deeply sentimental reasons for validation also. Validation and denial of validation by important other persons leads inevitably to reinterpretations of one's activity. Moreover, since not only we but the others are seeking to have judgments upheld in open court, and since validation is actively sought, it is no wonder that the "new is ever upspringing."[8]

Any classification is open to challenge and re-evaluation, by another or oneself. This is equivalent to saying that the errors of our ways are discovered in action. A certain amount of error can be calculated in advance on the basis of past experience. If all future situations were identical with past ones, then error would be at a minimum; like the carefully trained rat in the psychologist's maze, once the way was learned virtually no wrong responses could be made. But the future is uncertain, is to some extent judged, labeled and known after it happens. This means that human action necessarily must be rather tentative and exploratory. Unless a path of action has been well traversed, its terminal point is largely indeterminate. Both ends and means may be reformulated in transit because unexpected results occur. Commitment, even to a major way of life or destiny, is subject to revision in process—at least until the final commitment of self-sacrifice. Revision and re-evaluation are tantamount to admission of error. Men, from whose acts temporal categories cannot be separated, make constant mistakes in judging past, present, and future; their lives are marked by comedies and tragedies of error.

Danger and Dispossession

Error, re-evaluation, and the hypothetical nature of classifications, suggest a further corollary feature of man's relationship to his world. A thoroughly static environment, met with thoroughly stable responses, would be in turn thoroughly known. A problematic world presents not only discovery but danger. The danger consists in the possibility that one may lose his world and his possessions.

These losses are related. "To possess" connotes "to have," but the possession of objects means much more than merely having them around. Self-regard is linked with what is owned, with what is one's own. A man's possessions are a fair index of what he is, providing the observers take the trouble to distinguish what a man owns by chance and of what he is really endeared. It is no accident that men mark their symbolic movements—into social classes, for instance—by discarding and by acquiring clothes, houses, furnishings, friends, even wives. People willingly give away objects that no longer suit or fit, and the voluntary gift of a cherished possession signifies great regard for the person upon whom gift and regard are simultaneously conferred. Common speech indeed recognizes that a man may be so heavily identified with some of his properties as to be possessed by them; that is, he is so greatly involved with them that he is no longer quite himself. All this is not mere word play, for when crucial possessions are lost—by theft, fire, bungling, betrayal, or whatever—then also a man for a time may lose his way. Having lost his property, he may give up, and change purposes and path. Likewise, when a person changes his course, the meanings of his previous possessions change. In some subtle sense he loses them, although legally he may still own them.

However, the point I especially wish to stress is that a problematic world implies the continual danger of losing hold of objects into which great investments have been poured, objects with which we are heavily involved. A pet may die, a toy may be lost, and thus a household may be upset. This kind of loss is, perhaps, more obvious than the fact that people and relationships move out of possession also—indeed, must inevitably be lost if not continually repossessed. If identities are changing, if relationships are reconstituted by action; then anyone's possession of another person's regard or love or envy is impermanent. Camus has astutely remarked that "other people are always escaping us and we are always escaping them."[9] Final possession would mean death; it would mean to fix forever, like killing the person you love so that nothing can ever change or mar the relationship. People have been known to do this. The gist of all this is that involvements are evolvements—in the course of which parties and their relationships become trans-

formed. I shall say more about this when discussing interaction.

There are other facets of "loss of world" worth noting
here. Thus at the point where any man is questioning
certain important "me's" and finds that he does not know
quite how to characterize them, he is midstream between
danger and discovery. In some sense he is "alone" with his
experience, wrestling with something that is as yet uncom-
municable. There is a temporary, if minor, gap between
events and his understanding of them, and he is aware of
this gap. Under certain social conditions a man may undergo
so many or such critical experiences for which conventional
explanations seem inadequate, that he begins to question
large segments of the explanatory terminology that has
been taught him. In the internal rhetorical battle that ensues, his opponents may be conceived as lying or manipulating events to their own advantage, as wrong, or as duped.
But a man cannot question his own basic terminology without questioning his own purposes. If in large measure he
rejects the explanations he once believed, then he has been
alienated and has lost a world. He has been "spiritually dispossessed." If he embraces a set of counter-explanations or
invents a set of his own, then he has regained this world,
for the world is not merely "out there" but is also what
he makes of it.

Alienation and repossession generally are not occurrences
that happen merely to isolated sufferers, but simultaneously
to particular sectors of the population. Certain alienated
persons eventually discover that others are facing similar
problems and experiences, and the new terminologies arising
out of these discoveries are shared products. These take the
form of new philosophies, new interpretations of the world,
of situations, persons, and acts. Such radical transvaluation is
equivalent to new vision, a re-seeing of the meanings and

ends of human life. Some writers have remarked that such collective philosophies are really metaphors:

It makes a fundamental difference to our mode of life whether we look upon the world as something like a home, a station on the way home, a testing ground, an arsenal of potential tools, a quarry supplying material to the human workman, a foreign country, an enemy camp, or a prison. All these possibilities have been tried out at one time or another.[10]

In their working out of the new metaphor through new institutions and group activities, men encounter both challenge and danger. It is not surprising that some philosophers stress "discovery" and some stress "abyss."

Commitment and Self-Possession

Someone who has lost his world, or is experiencing great difficulty in retaining it, is commonly spoken of as having lost his way. This is tantamount to saying that his commitments—to significant others and to himself—have been tremendously weakened. When a man questions his central purposes, he is asking himself: to what, for what, to whom am I committed? You can discern this kind of questioning of yourself even in brief and mild bouts of self-doubt. The person who knows his world well, who is familiar with all its pathways, is strongly committed. Committed to what? To a conception of himself as a certain kind—or kinds—of person, who is expected to, and himself expects to, act in certain ways in certain situations. If the situations that arise are not entirely familiar, they are nevertheless somewhat like the old ones and demand similar lines of action.

Commitment, then, will involve conviction as to what is right and proper as well as their converse: what is worth striving for, fighting for, what is to be avoided, abhorred, considered cheap or sinful, and so on. Commitment in some acts may be slight, for one's action may be provisional, forced, or indifferently valued; but insofar as a line of action is assessed highly, then involvement is strong. Indulging in a play of words, we may note that to invest a man with an official position is to offer him the possibility of investing himself heavily in its enactment—so much so that he may be loathe to yield to the next candidate, having put so much of himself into the office. The dictionary definitions of "invest" reveal something of this tight complex of office, of donning symbolic clothing, of fealty or loyalty, contract or commitment, and self-involvement. To be deeply involved in a course of action is to "care," to be concerned, to be identified with it. As Kenneth Burke puts it, "action is not merely a means of doing but a way of being."[11]

This is thrown into especially sharp relief by two kinds of happenings, neither infrequent. Everyone has had the experience of using some kind of action as a means for a purpose, and then growing so interested in or fascinated with the means that it became of more concern than the original end. It can become, in fact, an important end in itself with which you can be identified to the depths of your being. The growth of involvement is also neatly illustrated by what may occur when you act without much conviction or strong identification, only to find that others assume that you really meant what you had done, that this act was really "you." You can disclaim your act, but if your motives are suspect, if the claim is discounted, then not only may you live with your act but come to repeat it with growing conviction.

A consideration of what it means to endeavor and to be dedicated should make still clearer the linkage between commitments and a sense of identity. Endeavor is continued action or enterprise, having to do with striving after certain values that the individual esteems. Since values are not purely individualistic matters, personal striving usually is shared enterprise. This is especially apparent when an individual has clearly responsible membership in groups possessing clear-cut goals. Insofar as he conceives of himself as an integral part of the group, he allies himself with progress toward its goals; its path to some extent becomes his own path, its failures his own failures. His dual commitment to the group and to himself can be quite "total" or complete as when a revolutionist or a religious sectarian rejects family, friendship, and other ties to throw himself wholly into the collective cause. Commitment—and conviction—of course is rarely so total since most persons have strong loyalties and obligations to more than one over-riding group.

Endeavor is not always associated with membership in well-organized groups. A man may be committed to his own career, usually related to family goals, or to the pursuit of his own fairly individualistic ends. Thus it has been said often that many Americans are dedicated to striving for monetary and social success; also that in the attainment of his goals, any artist is really on his own. It is true that ends can be sought individually, but scarcely individualistically. Notions of what constitute social or artistic success, how to get there, how to recognize benchmarks of progress, whom to emulate and spurn, how to display to significant others the current point of arrival—all of these are widely shared by other persons who are anything but isolated from one another, communicatively speaking.

In either case, long continued enterprise involves dedication and devotion—to utilize a religious but highly appropriate terminology. Anyone who has long been deeply involved with a group, a movement, will have expended considerable time and energy in pursuit of its goals. Dedication to individualistically oriented purposes involves equally durable motivation, and equally firm beliefs as to where one belongs—that is, what one is. To carry the reli-

gious metaphor further: any long standing commitment
means an agreement to sacrifice, however weak the commitment may be. Any group has the right to demand certain
sacrifices from its members. The individual makes like
demands upon himself, whether or not he is part of well
organized groups; as his own audience and judge he asks
himself not to dally along the roadside, not to give way to
temptations, and to give up some things but not to give
up his quest.

Sacrifice may quite literally involve any cherished thing,
act, or person. In some subtle sense, a cherished object is
one that belongs to its owner—although "own" is not necessarily synonymous with legal property rights—and with which
he feels identified. Dedication to some higher cause may
call for the abandonment even of those things with which
we are most identified, with which we are so deeply involved
that to part with them is almost to destroy ourselves: wives
and children, for instance.

The epitome of sacrifice, of course, is self-sacrifice or
motive unto death. One yields himself up—as if on a ritual
altar—so that his profoundest convictions and purposes may
be furthered. The self-sacrificial act is supra-individual, it
belongs to a larger and grander design which far transcends
a person's own impure motives. Hence it is not astonishing
that far from going to death reluctantly or with fear, voluntary martyrdom may be joyously sought. "Martyr" is
derived from the Greek word for "witness," a significant
etymological root. Though not always embraced with eager-
ness, martyrdom is accomplished by a tremendously vital
sense of mystical identification or union. By his act, the
martyr becomes "one with the higher cause" or "one with
the higher being." Self-sacrifice signifies often the firmest of
identities and the most total of commitments. There is no
holding back and no coming back. Unlike all other lines
of action, its consequences are final—this act is what it "is"

and not what it may seem to be upon future re-evaluation. To quote and then paraphrase John Dewey, "the thing actually at stake in any serious deliberation is . . . what sort of person is one to become, what sort of self is in the making"[12]—but the thing at stake in self-sacrifice is an irrevocable statement as to what one's self *is*. It is no wonder that around sacrifice, whether real or fictitious, myth and legend cluster. Sacrificial acts are exemplars pointing back to what was accomplished, and portents, signs, of what may yet be achieved in the way of a new identity.

What the new identity will be—for anyone, after any critical self-appraisal—no one can quite predict, including the person who is doing the self-appraising. Human careers, as I remarked in introducing this chapter, have always an unfinished character, a certain indeterminancy of outcome. Put thus directly, I fear the matter appears trite, something scarcely worth saying. Perhaps so: although people show amazing reserves—shocking as well as astonishing—even to friends who believe they know them minutely; and even the elderly frequently seem to refuse to obey the orderly rule of the bent twig. But this chapter has covered more terrain than a mere declaration that life is open-ended. It has stated the position that it is not change that needs to be explained but its specific directions; and it is not lack of change that needs to be taken for granted, but change itself. This latter point requires much more elaboration, as does the social patterning of personal continuity and discontinuity, and we shall undertake these tasks presently. I turn first to a consideration of some of the complexities of human interaction, taking as my major focus its symbolic and developmental character.

CHAPTER THREE

Interaction

THE student of identity must necessarily be deeply interested in interaction for it is in, and because of, face-to-face interaction that so much appraisal—of self and others—occurs. To be sure "interaction" is such a sufficiently ambiguous term as perhaps to signify no more than the encounters and interplay of persons. Various ways of viewing and analyzing interactional process are possible; and it will become quickly apparent that my way is directed by certain kinds of theoretical interests, derived mainly from my stance as a sociologist. I am not so much interested, for instance, in interpersonal process as are the psychiatrists. I am primarily interested in interaction that takes place between persons viewed as members of groups—however subtle the character ot their membership. Conventional, though effective, ways of analyzing interaction between and among members of "social positions" have been evolved by social scientists as they have sought to investigate and understand group and institutional structure. But a more detailed stare at the interactional process demands a more elaborate vocabulary, and a somewhat different viewpoint, if we would supplement and enrich our studies of social organizations and their members.

As a first step toward discussing interaction, I wish to direct your attention to "motivation." My treatment of the topic will not remind you very much of what is found in most social psychology textbooks or in psychoanalytic writings. I have been struck by something akin to an implicit motivational theory in many sociological research reports; and this has been more explicitly formulated by such men as George Mead, Kenneth Burke, C. Wright Mills, Alfred Lindesmith, and Nelson Foote.[1] The quotation from Schwartz and Stanton that closes this section on motivation should help to illustrate my point about an implicit theory of motivation. When the social scientist focuses upon interaction within institutional settings—as in hospitals or factories—he tends to write about the ways in which persons regard other persons, the motives that they attribute to each other, and he is interested in the consequences that flow from this special type of name-calling.

Motivation

The act of identifying objects, human or physical, allows a person to organize his action with reference to those objects. Such overt action may consist of a series of smaller acts which add up to a line of activity, as for instance when you identify your pen as having run dry. The whole sequence of actions—observing that the pen ceases to write, pressing harder to test whether any ink remains, testing further by opening the pen filler, then fetching the ink, filling the pen, wiping off the excess ink—constitutes the line of behavior "released" by your definition of the pen as "in need of ink." Note that in this illustration the line between "object" (dry pen) and "situation" (the pen has run dry) is largely semantic. In that sense behavior toward even physical objects is situational.

Elaborate sequences of acts likewise occur because you must identify social situations in order to cope with them. Consider the following mundane situation: a man enters his house at the end of the afternoon, kisses his wife who has come to the door to greet him, engages in a few conventional remarks, and sits down to listen to the radio newscast while his wife continues to prepare dinner. Sociologists would say that the situation was "well defined." Both man and wife identify the overall situation, recognize their agreed-upon division of labor, and know in general what preceded and what will follow. The myriad of cues striking their eyes and ears are perceived as conventionally named objects —living room, greetings, kiss. Many cues are not noticed, but those noticed tend to be relevant to performances within the domestic drama.

Implicit also in the organization of either participant's line of action is the assumption of each that the identities of both self and other are known. The husband sees or recognizes or defines or identifies or classifies—depending upon which verb one chooses to use—his wife and himself vis-a-vis each other in this sequence of familiar acts. Who and what she is and he is, so far as this situation is concerned, are not in question. This is not to say that all matters of reciprocal identity are settled, but only that each knows which of his and her possible identities—their possible "I's" —are likely to enter into this conventionally acted out situation.

Suppose now the husband arrives home as usual but finds a situation that he is unable to define satisfactorily, at least initially. For the sake of illustration suppose his wife's greeting lacks customary warmth and that she retires quickly without further speech. If this concatenation of gestures strikes him as unfamiliar, then he is faced with a problem of definition. A series of related questions—involving the proper identification of gestures, objects, events, persons and situation—must be answered.

Central to his inquiry and its satisfactory solution are questions relating to personal identity and to motives. Consider first the matter of identity. Of course, he knows who his wife "is" in a general sense; he knows her name, her general status (daughter, wife, mother), and her characteristic traits and gestures. What he does not know is in which of her capacities she is acting—and this he must discover. Is she sick, self-absorbed, angry, reproachful? If either of the latter, at or toward whom—me, her mother, her daughter, someone I do not know? If his wife's gestures are unusual or the situation which caused them is not easily identified, then the husband must search for cues in his memory, in the room. If her behavior is not entirely unfamiliar, then his recollection of similar situations, in conjunction with certain validating acts of his own, may quickly allow him to label "what is going on."

In a problematic situation, a person must not only identify the current other, he must *pari passu* identify his current self.

Establishment of one's own identity to oneself is as important in interaction as to establish it for the other. One's own identity in a situation is not absolutely given but is more or less problematic.[2]

"Who am I in this situation?" is problematic just as long as the situation is problematic. Identification of the situation depends upon making interlocked discriminations concerning relevant events, things, and persons—including oneself. All these must be discovered. Only with conventional activities is it possible instantly, effortlessly, almost automatically to read off the definition of the situation and all that the definition implies.

In the latter kinds of situations, the participants carry out required or expected sequences of acts. These are self-explanatory. They are understood by everyone involved as flowing from the nature of the situations and the conventional roles of participants. No one questions why a salesgirl returns to the customer his rightful change, and why he expects her to; or why a lifeguard slowly rows his boat at the edge of a swimming area. Explanations of such behavior exist, of course, but they have the status of assumptions rather than queries. It is different with problematic situations. Here, any person trying to define the situation is necessarily grappling also with motivational problems. You are forced to ask, by the very ambiguity of the situation, what do those acts mean? Why did those others perform them?

To answer necessitates that you ask such further detailed questions as who directed the act at whom? Why? Was it an act by itself, or did it follow something that others—perhaps I, myself—did or said? Or was it merely a segment of a longer act? You cannot answer such questions without having to decide what names to assign everybody in the particular drama—that is, their situational identities. But this categorization also requires you to judge their motives. The inferential character of all this is underlined by the mistakes, trifling or serious, that one may make in the naming of others' acts.

If participants in any situation did not make such assumptions or guesses about the grounds of others' action, their own action would be stymied, or at best exploratory. The imputation of motives to others is necessary if action is to occur. Like other designations, motivational assessments may be quite incorrect; nevertheless sequences of action will be organized in light of those assessments.

What does it mean to say that "motivational assessments may be quite incorrect"? Presumably, that there is some standard of correctness, that a man was so motivated and another man gave this and no other assessment of the motivation. Thus put, the matter seems simple; actually it is extremely complex. Let us refer back, first, to previous discussions of naming and classifying, since it is clear that assigning reasons for acts is essentially a matter of saying what these reasons and acts "are." Classifications are not "in" the object; an object gets classified from some perspective. The same object will be differently classified from different perspectives; and categories into which it can be placed are inexhaustible. Different groups of men have characteristic perspectives and so neither name objects identically nor possess exactly equivalent systems of classi-fication. All this is as true of events and acts as for things. In the words of C. W. Mills: "Men discern situations with particular vocabularies."[3]

With this in mind, consider now what must occur if two persons with vastly different social backgrounds meet. Their classifications of acts will only partially overlap. Suppose that one man acts and the other imputes a motive to his act. Frequently such an imputation will disagree with the actor's own understanding of what he has done; for though there is some overlap between their systems of naming, there is also much discrepancy. The motive attribution (by the observer) and the motive avowal (by the actor) will reflect this discrepancy. What each most certainly will do is to project into the other's behavior what might be his own reasons for acting. Most writers of historical romances capi-talize on this propensity to project, so that 18th century characters are really "out of character" because their deeds are actuated by the motives of our own century. You will recall that Mark Twain revised this standard formula and placed a Connecticut Yankee in King Arthur's Court, much of the humor and plot of his story turning upon the diffi-culties which beset the pretender.

The historical romance parodies the real problem of ob-taining consistency between the motivational attribution of observers and the motivational avowal of the characters themselves, were the latter alive. Few readers of these ro-mances may question the author's motivational imputations, but this does not certify the author's accuracy. Likewise, in real life, agreement among any group of people concerning the motives of another person merely tells us something about the common terminology with which they operate; in fact, it would be surprising if persons who used much the same explanatory vocabulary did not arrive frequently at much the same judgments.

The search for motives is, as we have seen, a search for an answer to a query. If your answer seems satisfactory, then you can organize your own action, taking the other person thus into account. If consequences ensue as expected, then your assessment tends to be confirmed. Even when consequences are not quite anticipated, they can be set aright by a kind of explanation piled upon explanation, as when it is said that the other's act looks like one thing but is *really* underneath, in somewhat disguised form, the kind that was anticipated.

(Thus the attribution of motives to resident doctors by medical students—who are likely to feel underprivileged in the teaching hospital, and as though they are made to do the residents' dirty work—is an attribution, negative in tone, that evolves only as a result of considerable and continual student discussion and because the acts of residents are frequently ambiguous, thereby in need of interpretation. The field worker on the study, from which this observation is drawn, often attributed other, more benign, motives to the residents; noting that the students ignored or explained away cues that led to his own different imputations.) [4]

Your own motives also are matters of query and inquiry to yourself except in those regulated circumstances where actions are duly prescribed as if by a social script. But as I noted some paragraphs ago, the placement of identities in undefined situations also involves questions of self placement; that is, not only who am I in this situation, but what have I done that is relevant to the situation and what shall I do that will be appropriate to both the situation and the motives of the other persons? The relevant answers are not always lucidly or explicitly vocalized or systematically worked out, but some interpretation, some acts of designation must occur. Part and parcel of any interpretation of a situation is an interpretation of how one has behaved and is about to behave. This last set of interpretations can be termed a motivational statement.[5] It embodies a justification of the overt behavior that follows upon its formulation in terms of "more or less anticipated consummations and consequences."[6]

An unkind critic may say that the justification is an afterthought, a rationalization, a set of plausible reasons to satisfy others who might ask "why did you act as you did?" Often the reasons that you will give are not those that you know to be true. You are making a distinction between the explanation you give the public and the explanation you give yourself. Such a public avowal is equivalent to misnaming the act deliberately. A genuine motivational statement is not intended to deceive anyone. It is the person's summation, given to himself and only incidentally to others if he should choose to tell them, of what he is about to do and why. It involves "an estimation of the consequence of one's acts and an evaluation of these effects."[7] For instance, "given the necessity of staying in school, and my bad marks, and the probability that this good student next to me won't protest, I'll copy, with a good chance of getting away with it."

What is the distinction then, if any, between a motivational statement and the overt action which follows? It is clear that they are not separate units, like a hand which throws a ball. The verbal (spoken to oneself, or more usually, merely thought) statement is an integral part of the entire activity. The act does not begin with its overt expression, the motivational statement merely preceding or accompanying the visible motions. Assessment of situation, persons, and self enter into the organization of an act, and are part of its structure.

There is not always a separation between public and private justifications. The justification that I offer myself is not entirely unique, individualistic, or generally anti-social. Because I learn to perceive and judge within socializing surroundings, and because I must take into account other persons' evaluations of my justifications, my public and private avowals often show no discrepancies. As Mills says:

To term them justifications is *not* to deny their efficacy. Often anticipations of acceptable justifications will control conduct. . . . In many social actions, others must agree, tacitly or explicitly. Thus, acts often will be abandoned if no reason can be found that others will accept.[8]

Motive avowal and motive imputation are not radically different acts; they differ only insofar as motives are assigned to myself or to others. But the only motives that can be imputed are those which I myself can understand. I cannot attribute to others, any more than to myself, motives not dreamed of; neither can I attribute motives that I place no credence in, as for instance compacts with the devil or secret possession by spirits. We use the vocabularies of motive which we have learned to use, whether on ourselves or on others. When a man comes into contact with groups new to him and thus learns new terminologies, his assignments of motive become affected. He learns that new kinds of motivation exist, if not for himself then for others. Having admitted that such grounds for action do exist, it is often but a step to ascribe them to himself.

At this juncture it may very well be protested that I have been discussing the assignment of motives, but what about the real or actual motives? Is not the crux of the matter the *actual* motive, the one that is really operative? As the psychoanalysts have taught us, this is not easy to know, least of all if the motives are our own.

Since my aim is to discuss motives here only within the context of interaction, I wish only to point out that any social scientists attempting to get at the real root of an act must go through essentially the same procedures as the layman, but with more care, caution, and sophistication. If the meaning of some act, or set of acts, is obscure or uncertain—as when an adolescent is continually sarcastic to his mother—then the scientist proceeds to gather data. These may be of various kinds depending upon the interests, training, and perspicacity of the particular scientist, and may include the motivational statements of each member of the family, observations of the child and the mother, batteries of psychological tests, school records, and information about social class. After a considered judgment of the assembled data, a judgment of the child's grounds for action can reasonably be made. The terminology with which the scientist approaches problematic acts is marked by its systematic organization, and in this it differs from many non-scientific vocabularies. But the technical terms, like all other systems of classification, embody conceptions of what the world and its men essentially are. I am not concerned with the accuracy of the scientist's assessment, but with indicating how, like the layman's, it affects interaction between the scientist and "the other." The relationship here is not obscure; when a psychiatrist believes he understands his patient's basic motivations, or immediate motivations, he attempts to act in accordance with that assessment. A much more subtle instance, with many institutional ramifications, is suggested by Schwartz and Stanton in their fine study of a ward in a mental hospital.

The most common, most conspicuous, and most clearly serious misunderstanding occurred when someone, staff member or patient, ignored the explicit meaning of a statement or action and focused attention on an inferred meaning. This was a very frequent failing of seriously schizophrenic patients; its results were, curiously, to give rise to the belief that such patients might have an almost mysterious intuition. It was an equally frequent failing of the psychiatrists, so frequent as to amount almost to an occupational illness. . . .

. . . patients with paranoid trends . . . found themselves thoroughly at home in such an environment and contributed heavily to its maintenance. . . .

Restriction of attention to "deep" interpretation was not . . . confined to dealing with patients; on the contrary, many psychiatrists seemed to pride themselves on ignoring the face value of what their colleagues said to them, focusing instead on what they believed to be "really going on." . . . information was frequently lost . . . particularly when a junior staff member protested to a senior about certain aspects of the hospital; the protest was likely to be interpreted as a transference rebellion. This interpretation was rarely made when the younger staff member agreed with the older. Because of these pseudo-deep interpretations, communication sometimes became so complex that the situation could almost be summarized by the statement, "If you disagree with me, you need to see a psychiatrist." . . .

We have mentioned that these misunderstandings may be long lasting. This is true when the mechanics of the misunderstanding include self-confirming processes. . . . Many schizophrenic patients tend . . . to become incoherent when confronted with . . . a "deep" interpretation without adequate preparation. Now, if the psychiatrist or staff member interprets this very incoherence as confirming evidence of his interpretation, as many do, he often feels actually obligated to try in every possible way to "make the patient see" what "is really going on" by "facing her with it." When this happens, the misunderstanding can continue indefinitely. Similarly, the young staff member whose protest is interpreted as rebellion against the "father figure," is likely to drop it while he attempts "to work out" the problem in his own treatment; during this usually prolonged period of silence, the physician who made the interpretation of a transference phenomenon is likely to find his opinion confirmed by this very silence. Both staff members lose sight of the fact that the actual cogency of the protest has not been dealt with.[9]

Face-to-Face Interaction: Complex and Developmental

The consequences of motivational imputation for interaction in the hospital are impressive; but we dare not confine analysis of interaction merely to motivation, for it involves much more than the need to attribute motives to others and to oneself. First of all, it will pay us to recognize the tremendous complexity of interaction and to see in detail some of the specific events that make it so complex; this in turn will contribute toward our understanding of its developmental, or evolving, quality.

Face-to-face interaction is a fluid, moving, "'running" process; during its course the participants take successive stances vis-a-vis each other. Sometimes they fence, sometimes they move in rhythmic psychological ballet, but always they move through successive phases of position. The initial reading of the other's identity merely sets the stage for action, gives each some cues for his lines. Events may turn out as expected; nonetheless an astute observer can notice a groundbase of unwitting interplay and often witting by-play.

For certain purposes it may suffice to describe interaction as going on between persons who each enact a role or occupy a status. The actors, then, are said to perceive the situation, observe what is required with respect to the status of each, and carry out the requisite or selected line of action. For discussion of events that occur between representatives of certain social positions, this kind of description is often adequate, but for our purposes, it is not. The adoption of a general role (say, lawyer giving advice) toward a person of a given status (client) merely suggests the general framework within which interplay will go on. The lawyer, of course, will observe various boundaries of decorum, will act according to his general conceptions of professional rights and obligations. But awareness of position enters into interaction in tremendously subtle ways. Actors "enact their roles"—but how? The terms "enact" or "act out a role" suggest but do not come to grips with the complexity and phase-like character of interplay, nor do they emphasize the frequently unexpected results of interactional drama. The model of role-enactment interaction, however, provides a useful jumping-off place for considering what does happen when two people are talking and gesturing face-to-face.

To begin with the term "interaction" tends to obscure the fact that much more than two flesh and blood persons are responding to one another. If we were to use a playwright's imagery, we would say that although there are only two main actors on the stage, there are also other actors who are visible only to the audience, or to one or the other of the main actors. Thus, each of the actors, while acting toward the other, may also be acting toward an invisible third, much as if the latter were actually present. To make the matter more complicated, if actor A is officially representing a group with respect to actor B then in a real sense the entire group should be there upon the stage, so that when A makes a commendable statement they will nod in collective approval, and then A will as much respond to them as to B. Or A may view B as representing a group that he dislikes, so B should be standing with his group ranged about him.

If we wish to approach the complexity of real interactional events, we would also have to make arrangements for the supplementary actors to make exits and entrances and to fade in and out of the immediate circle of conversation when they were and were not relevant to the main drama. Their visibility might be signalized by their donning and doffing appropriate masks. These supplementary actors will represent a wide range of relationships: relatives, friends, teachers, and so on. Some will be persons long since dead, or arising out of the actor's past. Many will represent groups to which the actor belongs, and will expect appropriate gestures from him during the interaction. Some of the invisible actors will be legends and myths which enter the drama and effect the action of the main human actors. The interactional situation is not an interaction between two persons, merely, but a series of transactions carried on in thickly peopled and complexly imaged contests.

Some of these transactions consist of each person's responses to himself. It would be well here to recollect Reizler's remark that the "I" can respond to many "me's": among them the me of yesterday, tomorrow, several minutes ago, the me of the immediate present, and the me in general. In face-to-face situations, persons respond to various facets of themselves and their performances. For instance, you may be surprised and shocked that you have just said what you did, and quickly make amends. You may feel guilt at a remark and respond covertly to your guilt without your listener knowing of this. During the course of conversation, you may catch a clear image of what you "really" said several minutes ago, and respond to that picture. You may be so pleased at an immediately preceding conversational maneuver that you respond spontaneously to it—say, with a smile of self-satisfaction—but without realizing that your response is visible and possibly significant to the other. Furthermore, you may revise your act immediately after its inception because you respond quickly to its expression and direction.

Just as the "me" (or self-object) can be various, so may the responses of the "I" (or acting subject). I can explode quickly, without reflection, at one of my own responses. I can dimly experience feelings about my performance without being clear what exactly I am experiencing. And—to take a more complicated response—I can note how my interpretation of the other's role in the situation is proving to be correct and very carefully guide my next response thereby, while simultaneously congratulating myself upon my astute judgment. All such responses to myself and to him enter as part of the interactional process, and it must be remembered that all participants are behaving thus. Since some of the other's responses to himself take visible form, these provide suggestive indexes to me of what is going on "inside" him;

and to miss or misread such signs is to do so at risk to comfort, security, and success.

The responses made to one's self probably are not so very
different—at least in certain ways—than are the responses
directed to others. You may respond to the other covertly
or visibly; explosively or with temperance and prudence;
after an articulate judgment or spontaneously "without
thinking" to the tones and the rhythms of his voice. You may
often be unaware of the full complement of your responses
to him, precisely as he may be unaware or dimly aware of
the full measure of his own response to himself. Just as you
cannot observe everything about yourself while in action, you
cannot possibly perceive everything about another person.

To be unaware or dimly aware of such responses—whether
to yourself or to him—does not necessarily signify that you
have repressed actual knowledge of them. You may fail to
"see" certain gestures made by the other because you lack
the appropriate categories or the appropriate training to
perceive them. You may fail to notice certain gestures or
tones because you are thinking about, or noticing, other
things. You may notice certain gestures only dimly because
they seem unimportant, or do not appear relevant to some
hypothesis that you are entertaining about the other's behavior. Of course, you may avoid noticing persistently, if
unwittingly, certain events because to note them would
arouse your anxiety; but it is not necessary to assume that
all, or even most, unawareness must be accounted for on
such repressive grounds.

However, the point at issue here is not so much the causes
of unawareness as the important point that the interactional
course is due in considerable part to unwitting responses
made by each participant. Consider that in any single instant any one of the following may happen: (1) A may respond quite consciously to a witting gesture of B's; (2) A
may respond consciously to an unwitting response of B's (a

tone of voice or a movement of a hand) ; (3) A may respond without himself being aware of his response to a conscious response of B's; (4) A may respond unwittingly to an unwitting response of B's. Now double these points by substituting B for A and A for B. This picture is further complicated by the fact that each participant can respond so immediately to the other's tones, speech rhythms and gestures that his own response is unconscious when it is made, but thoroughly conscious afterward; either because he then notes it himself, or because it is pointed out to him by the other's answering actions.

In such tremendously complicated interplay, there is ample room for both actors to make errors of judgment. A classification, however crude, of reactions to self and other will help isolate dimensions along which error and accuracy of judgment may occur. Each person has the tasks of assessing about the other (1) his general intent in the situation, (2) his response toward himself, (3) his responses or feelings toward me, the recipient or observer of his action. These three tasks are interrelated, but are not necessarily identical nor do they call identical observational skills into play. It seems entirely possible that I might be more accurate about sensing feelings expressed toward me, in a given interactional situation, than in comprehending the other person's responses to himself—or vice versa. Certainly also I may grasp his general intent, particularly when he makes an effort to display it, but at many specific moments during the interaction I may commit errors about his reaction to me as well as his reaction to himself. Thus, in an experimental role-drama, a husband understood what his wife was trying to get him to do, but badly misjudged her feelings toward him, both in general and at particular moments, and also misread her reactions toward her own remarks. The interpretational interweaving of signs of intent, signs of self-feeling, and signs of feelings expressed toward me, must be exceedingly complex. For example, I may hypothesize about intent from the other person's initial gambit, and later verify or revise my notions as I read further signs that suggest his immediate feelings toward me. Conversely, my judgments of how he is currently responding to me, or toward himself, rest upon some notion of his general intent in the situation.

What is often loosely referred to as "taking the role of the other" must include all such phases and processes of observation and inference, although the phrase scarcely does more than point up how little is actually known about these processes other than common sense observation. (Ralph Turner's recent analysis of "role-taking" turns about distinctions similar to those just presented. Turner discriminates between taking the other's attitude toward myself; and taking his attitude toward anyone else, including presumably himself. Turner also distinguishes among the standpoints from which I may view the other's attitude: from my own standpoint, from a third party's, and from that of the other person himself. Turner terms this last standpoint, "identifying.") [10]

The three tasks concerned with assessing the other's responses surely are paralleled by the necessity for assessing one's own responses. This might, somewhat facetiously, be termed "taking the role of myself."[11] At the risk of belaboring the point, note that everyone has also to interpret his own responses; their meanings are far from self-evident. Much that I have said about the difficulties that prevent correct interpretation of the other's responses is quite applicable to my own. Elements of self-delusion, avoidance of anxiety and of attack on self-esteem slant the observation of self, but probably not very differently from the way they enter to obscure observation of others. Taking the viewpoint of the other and taking the viewpoint of one's self are interrelated and complex processes. It would be a grievous error to suppose that because in interaction the behavior of other people is so often puzzling, you necessarily know how and why you yourself are acting.

Interaction, as I have described it, appears to be a fantastically complex web of action and counteraction. It *is* complex: and there is a point in stressing its complexity. A scientific vocabulary fashioned along the lines of "cues" or "stimulus and response" or "the unconscious" or "needs and drives" or merely "role-playing" and "status" and "self-conceptions" will tend to bypass rather than handle its intricacies. However, the complex picture that I have portrayed requires qualification in several ways.

Probably it is most unusual, during any one situation or at any one moment, for a person to be noting every aspect of interaction sketched above. Sometimes you are focused mainly upon your own psychological navel and pay little attention to the other's responses. At other times, your own responses are scarcely noticed, while his intent is deemed of very great importance. Focuses of attention necessarily shift; you cannot look everywhere at once. Even trained observers surely must miss a great deal on this account. Then again, in many situations a great many aspects of interaction are taken for granted, are conventionalized, and the focus of attention is directed, so to speak, by the participants' understandings of what the situation is all about. Two scientists excitedly conversing about a common abstract problem are likely to notice very little, indeed, of the purely personal aspects of the conversation. Furthermore, since people vary by training and background in the ways that they notice events, they must vary in their sensitivity to different aspects of interaction. It is probable that some people, or groups of people, respond typically and very consciously to speech rhythms, to innuendo, to contradictions of what is said, and to how it is said; while others react, at least consciously, mainly to what is said, and discriminate much less finely tone and affect. Possibly some people scarcely observe themselves "objectively," while it is certain that others are typically very self-conscious about observing themselves.

Until now I have often referred to interaction as if it were composed of a series of moments. But face-to-face interplay is better conceived as a narrative or dramatic process. It may not "go anywhere," nothing much may get accomplished, yet it proceeds by phases, by successions, however unaware the participants may be of moving through them. Anyone, if he wishes, can observe this phase-like, sometimes even plot-like, quality of his interactions. Conversations take a different turn. Natural cessation points are reached, control of the conversation passes from one actor to the other. Opening gambits are made in which persons test each other and then move on to other conversational maneuvers. These are all instances of what Herbert Blumer[12] has termed very accurately the "developing character" or "variable career" of interaction.

What interactional phases signify, of course, is that relations between the actors are changing, if only temporarily. But when the interaction goes somewhere, does not merely meander through phases, there occurs a genuine evolvement or development of relationships between the actors. As Blumer notes: "the transaction is other than the addition of the actions of two individuals; the two lines of action in their developing interrelationships constitute a singleness."[13] In this sense, an entire evening's conversation also can be considered as merely one phase in a developing relationship; so also can a short, sharp and dramatic interchange of remarks. After certain interchanges, there is quite literally "no return." A realignment is called for—and often is already there, announced, symbolized by the verbal and gestural exchange.

Even when interaction is fleeting, occasional, it is likely to have a cumulative and developmental character—as between a woman and her grocer. When persons interact "emotionally," "deeply," the cumulative character is more obvious. Then there is involvement; and as we noted when discussing possession and being possessed, an involvement is also an evolvement. But the matter is yet more complicated; for instance, both parties may be deeply involved with each other, or only one with the other. If the latter, then although their "interrelationships constitute a singleness," to quote Blumer again, there are many more phases, aspects, complexities for the person who has the greater investment in the relationship. Even when both parties are strongly committed to the relationship, each standing to the other as a highly significant other, the developmental tempi probably ought to be regarded as subtly dissonant and "off-beat." That is, since the meanings of the interaction differ for each in some or many regards, the realignments of relationship and grasp of phases will proceed at a somewhat different pace for each partner. Hence the development can be viewed from the standpoint of each, as well as from that of an outsider who is privy to both sides.

The development of self-other involvement proceeds not only by phases and gradual movement; it advances by spurts and unevenly paced movement. Anyone who has fallen in love, grown to hate an enemy, or found a friend will quickly recognize that although some of the evolvement was gradual, certain high points, certain events, occurred after which "we were closer" or "further." After these events, one is a different person to the other, and he is different to you, although precisely in what ways you cannot always say, nor may you know perhaps until further transactions with the other take place. But of equal significance: if the other is highly significant to you, if you really care about what he thinks of you and you of him, then after the crucial event you can become a different person to yourself. These critical junctures in interpersonal relationships can constitute turning points in self-regard.

Allow me now to sum up the remarks of the last few pages. We have taken a microscopic look at interaction. Because our interest in this essay is directed at personal identity, it was inevitable that we should focus upon the play of "me and you"; and that the developmental aspects of interaction should jump to the forefront of attention. There are modes of viewing interaction that conceive of it as more static, more as performance that goes to completion, or as simply problem solving with closure. For some purposes, it is certainly useful to so regard some interactional processes. It is also useful to regard them more specifically as occurring within the context of institutions or ordered group relations—and I shall do so presently. Before doing so, it will be useful to explore a special facet of me-you and me-other relationships that was implied in the foregoing discussion. Let me now make it explicit, albeit the discussion constitutes a slight digression from my main line of exposition.

Fantasy and Interaction

Fantasy, like reasoned thought or impulsive action, can be regarded as taking place within a context of interaction: it arises out of and has consequences for the encounters among people. I choose to discuss fantasy rather than more fragmentary covert processes (such as visual and auditory images or spontaneous visual recollections) because undeniably these latter do accompany and influence the course of conversations. Fantasy and reverie seem further removed from the course of action, and less likely to occur during conversational interplay; although, of course, when more than two persons are engaged in conversation, the third may withdraw long enough to play out an internal drama. My general position is this: fully conscious thinking directs action during, after, and preceding interaction, and so also do less reasoned mental processes.

"Fantasy" is easily and popularly equated with the unreal, the playful, the make-believe, the phantasmagoric; and "thought" with abstraction, logic, problem solving, or at least with the handling of a real world and real human relations. By some psychiatrists and psychologists, reverie, fantasy, daydreaming—whatever the terms—are conceived of as useful mainly because they are adjustive mechanisms; they are wish-fulfilling, or compensatory, or allow release of tension, or momentary escape from reality. When one protests, as has Robert Faris that fantasy is "preparation for hypothetical activity rather than . . . consummation,"[14] he is forced—because of the long existing dichotomy between thought and fantasy in Western conceptions—to make a case for the latter. One never need to make out a case for thought! This is exactly like the necessity for arguing the human usefulness of play (unreal activity) as over against work (real activity); and doubtless the parallel polarities have similar historical origins.

Suzanne Langer has written passionately and wisely of "man's ceaseless quest for conception and orientation," including very primitive forms such as ritual which she speaks of as "the most primitive reflection of serious thought, a slow deposit, as it were, of people's imaginative insight into life."[15] In joining ritual with thought she eradicates, or at least minimizes, the frequently made opposition of reason and irrationality, thought and fantasy. Her formulation forces attention to a whole range of related imaginative processes that have to do with, as she says, "conception and orientation." We need not think of these as entering human interaction merely in bizarre or negative, or even emotionally, expressive ways.

The types of daydreams, and their consequences upon interaction, must be legion. I once spent a number of hours interviewing people about their most recent day-dreams and am willing to hazard some guesses about how "private" fantasies funnel into public—and even institutional—interaction. Elsewhere Alfred Lindesmith and I have emphasized that "interaction between humans is dramatic in character, and . . . a dramatic imagery is required for both actual and imaginative participation in it."[16] Some fantasies directly affect this participation, others appear to do so much less directly. As with children, the line between adult daydreaming and "doing" is sometimes very slight: for instance, college instructors who are new to teaching sometimes daydream elaborate dramas in which they speak to their classes. This is one way to discover how to give the lecture and what to say and not to say.

A common kind of daydream is preparatory: you imagine how an encounter will work out. If it is important enough, you may play the scene several times, much like a movie director will repeat his scenes. If it has no other consequence, this probably eliminates alternative lines of action: for daydreaming is embedded not only in contexts of visual images, recollection, and internal dialogue, but often in contexts of self-judgments made upon daydreaming and its imagined outcomes. If you watch yourself closely, you can catch yourself trying out and discarding imagined encounters, including how you will arrange room settings and what you or the other will say first to some of the remarks or exchanges that will be made.

Other daydreams seem rather less frankly preparatory than aids toward imagining the content of some situation as yet vaguely conceived. "What will it be like when I get there?" is perhaps less a matter of trying out lines of action than it is an attempt to fill in the outlines of the unfamiliar future situation. It is probable that all passage into new kinds of status, when they are not precisely known, will be accompanied and preceded by such fantasies.

Reveries about the past occur, of course, and one kind consists of re-playing certain encounters to make them conso-

nant with what might have been done, or with what you
would now have done. Insofar as you pass judgment upon
these imaginary scenes it is probable that identity and future
action are sometimes affected, particularly if the issue fantasied about is sufficiently important. I suggest, also, apropos
of an earlier discussion of "reseeing" the past, that people
can be counted upon to daydream so as to bring their pasts
into line with their presents.

Occasionally daydreaming is swift and may occur even during an episode of interaction. A respondent once reported
that he was annoyed during a train ride by a talkative traveling companion. Throughout an interchange he felt like
smashing the man to bits and fantasied a quick short scene
in which he finally did just that. This eased his tension and
enabled him to endure with more tolerance the incessant
chattering. Perhaps, the more elaborately fantastic reveries
function in this way to relieve tension—as well as to sustain
and arouse it—but we can view them also as removing the
dreamer from interaction, as delaying interaction, and presumably sometimes as affecting the interaction that follows
the fantasy.

All these are individual daydreams but others are collective since two or more persons may participate in each
other's reverie process. Married couples who plan to build
a house, or to take a vacation, may do this. In the literal
sense, each does his own daydreaming; but conversation follows so closely upon the dreaming, setting off the talking
or dreaming of each, that the whole can be called "collective"
without stretching the term unduly. Charles Bolton,[17] who
is studying "falling in love," has suggested to me that a
similar process of conversationally shared reveries may sometimes occur. This kind of communication surely also occurs
at longer range through letters. Some collective reveries undoubtedly eventuate in "real" as well as purely affective action. Couples presumably purchase houses on the basis of

shared reveries and its associated planning. Teenagers engage in pranks after stimulating one another through conversation in which, no doubt, reveries are immediately shared.

Fantasy enters into the stream of face-to-face interaction in more institutionalized—hence less direct—fashion. The instance of the "vision," as experienced by young Indian males making passage into adulthood, is instructive here. Note that at a certain age, designated persons—but only those persons—are allowed to have visions; indeed, they are supposed to have visions. In later years they may have additional visions, or may not, depending upon the rules of the societal game. These institutionalized fantasies take place, usually, in prescribed places and at more or less prescribed times. Much of their content, like ordinary daydreaming, is set by the dreamer's immersion in a commonly shared culture, although the specific vision is experienced as an individual affair. Among some tribes, he must keep its contents secret, but in others he may seek advice on how to interpret it, either immediately or later in his life. There are rules governing who is allowed to interpret the vision, and who may not; to whom he can "in good form" tell it, and to whom he must not. The interpretation of the vision, in some measure at least, affects the future action of the man as a member of the tribe. It may yield him a mandate or a command to act in a generalized way, and it may give or confirm a sense of identity.

Let us extend this notion of the vision to any fantasy, and to any product of sets of fantasies, such as a poem, a painting, or a religious revelation. We are asking who has the right to fantasy, when, and in what fashion, and who has the right—and possibly the obligation—to interpret the fantasy, and to whom? In non-institutionalized fantasies, the same person necessarily performs both activities—although he may ask someone else to help interpret. Persons of certified status are authorized to interpret certain kinds of fantasies or the products of fantasies. Psychiatrists and psychoanalysts are authorized to do this. Elsewhere, soothsayers are licensed to interpret the visions of their clients as well as to make public their own. Prophets have had to fight against entrenched institutions in order to gain the right to have significant fantasies and to expound them in public. Established religious orders are faced constantly with spontaneous miracles claimed to be envisioned by lay members; the institutional problem is whether to deny their claimed status, and if not, then to enforce the right to define precisely their meaning. If the parallels seem not too far fetched: there is a division of labor in artistic worlds whereby certain persons, themselves not artistically skilled, earn the right to interpret the products of those who are skilled; and in the world of ideas, some persons, known as "idea men," are surrounded by others who are more gifted at developing or testing ideas. If you do not apply too rigidly the line between thought and fantasy, but conceive of creative endeavor as encompassing a great range of covert mental processes, then the point will not appear overdrawn.

In brief, I am declaring both that fantasy can be a very public, and regulated, matter, and that sometimes fantasy merely affects directly the course of face-to-face interaction between individuals. Viewed this way, the range of covert processes—variously denoted by the terms "reverie," "fancy," "daydreaming," and "fantasy"—are important for the conservation and change of identities. I have stressed the innovative aspects of fantasy processes rather than the conservative; and have related them to interaction rather than described or analysed them in great detail *per se*.

Structured Interactional Process

Now I return to consider what appear to be alternative ways of analysing interaction. Each of these is based upon a different scholarly tradition. Two predominant ways of studying interaction today are the psychiatric and the sociological. By contrasting these, and then elaborating the latter, certain other characteristics of interaction can be underscored.

Psychiatrists tend to conceive of interaction as carrying a heavy freight of personal imagery. Although the actors are also regarded as enacting conventional roles (e.g., father or son), the psychiatrist is considerably more interested in the "interpersonal relations" of the participants than in their enactment of culturally assigned positions. H. S. Sullivan puts it this way:

. . . besides the interpersonal situation as defined within the awareness of the speaker, there is a concomitant interpersonal situation quite different as to its principal . . . tendencies of which the speaker is more or less completely unaware.

Besides the . . . psychiatrist and subject there is . . . also an illusory group . . . of psychiatrist-distorted-to-accommodate-a-special-'you'-pattern and subject-reliving-an-earlier-unresolved-[experience]-and-manifesting-the-corresponding-special-'me'-pattern. The shift of communicative processes from one to another of these . . . may be frequent or only occasional; in any case, the alertness of the speaker is usually sufficient to insure the weaving of word patterns and other linguistic elements into grammatical speech. There, therefore, ensues an apparently coherent discussion, and one usually rather clearly addressed to the hearer.[18]

Sociologists generally put more social structure into the interaction: their attention is given to persons as members of social groups and organizations. Persons become role-players rather than individuals. Two persons in interaction are never merely persons but group representatives; a teacher and a student, of given social classes, ages, cliques, and the like. When sociological analysis becomes relatively complex, then the sequential enactment of a person's many memberships may be studied. If analysis becomes more complex yet, then the more or less simultaneous interplay of their audiences may be discussed; an example is Neal Gross' discovery that school superintendents had not one audience but many (students, teachers, school board, other superintendents), and that all or some of these might be relevant to what the superintendent said or did at any given moment.[19] But sociological analysis, as I remarked at the outset of this chapter, is less concerned with interaction as a detailed process than with the outcomes and products of interaction. My summation is oversimplified but is more or less accurate. (In small group research, which has developed during the last decade, interactional process is studied directly, usually under laboratory conditions. Who initiates contact, who receives it, how frequently, what is its nature, who talks most and in what order and what about: these are the kinds of items that are studied in relation to such matters as group solving and group cohesion. The focus of this interest in interaction is rather different from my own.)

It is useful to visualize interaction as both structured, in the sense that the participants represent social positions; and at the same time as not quite so structured. I shall develop my argument by beginning with an observation by E. C. Hughes[20] that the person who represents a given status is supposed to possess one or more attributes such as skills, certificates, and even certain age. In addition some other attributes may be expected and indeed required, although no one says so openly. Thus American physicians are required to possess necessary skills and training but also, more covertly, are supposed to be men and white-skinned. Hughes remarks that certain "dilemmas of status" flow from violation of the auxiliary aspects of status: for instance, a Negro doctor sets problems not only for white patients but for his white colleagues. The sharing of secondary qualifications allows people of the same status to work together familiarly and with relative ease and lack of embarrassment; whereas when some of these qualifications are missing, or certain others are present, the interaction is upset. A woman physician in a clinic staffed otherwise with male physicians changes the atmosphere. Her presence is apt to place a damper upon masculine jokes, and to evoke sexual byplay. Conversely, into the working relationship of nurse and doctor certain sexual overtones enter, including female subordination and male superordination, which a male nurse disturbs.

Suppose now we work out—while retaining Professor Hughes' concepts of overt and covert attributes—some possible combinations of status that may prevail during an encounter between doctors without concerning ourselves whether the encounter is disturbed or not. A male doctor can act at different moments in at least three capacities: as a doctor, a male, and a male doctor. If, now, female physicians are introduced into the picture, we have the following simple possibilities of interaction between any two physicians in the hospital setting:

	male phys.	male only	phys. only	female only	fem. phys.
male physician	. . .	. . .	. . .	. . .	. . .
male only	. . .	. . .	. . .	. . .	. . .
physician only	. . .	. . .	. . .	. . .	. . .
female only	. . .	. . .	. . .	. . .	. . .
female physician	. . .	. . .	. . .	. . .	. . .

Actually, one or more combinations may pertain during the entire span of an interaction. Which basis for relationship is operative during an interaction is problematic since more than one is always theoretically, and often practically, possible. The selection of bases is, in institutions like hospitals, related to questions of power and influence. The chief bases of interaction may have to be carefully prepared for and even forcefully impressed upon the personnel, when unusual status attributes are introduced, as when Negro nurses first started to work in white hospitals. In less formal contexts, people may nonetheless choose, with great awareness or with none.

When combinations that control interplay are simple—

such as doctor to doctor, doctor to male, male to female—then the course of the interaction is relatively simple and one-dimensional. However, it is more realistic to say that the mode of interaction can change at any instant or phase of interaction and not remain the same through its entire duration. That this is not a fictitious possibility is attested by the careful, ritualistic preparations for the confinement of interaction during conventional but socially precarious episodes, as when female patients are examined by male physicians. It is precisely then that other statuses—like race, age, and class—must be carefully controlled less the interaction founder upon revulsion, embarrassment, and other irrelevant reactions. (In the study of medical students previously mentioned, the field worker observed at the obstetrics clinic one woman's embarrassment, as she took her womanhood too literally during her examination. Conversely one student who was new to the routines of this clinic remarked that he had occasionally to leave a patient "until my symptoms go away"; but the assembly line character of obstetric treatment and delivery, plus the normal medical perspective of the medical student, probably makes this latter kind of reaction ordinarily either quickly passé or prevents its occurrence entirely.) Undoubtedly there are male physicians who are also homosexuals: we may be sure that their homosexuality ordinarily is kept covert during the examination of male patients, even if actively awakened at specific moments of physical contact.

To make the picture more realistic, if more complex: any man operating as an institutional representative may act during any interaction, or interactional phase, in several different institutional capacities: for instance, as a physician, an oculist, a chief of the clinic, an old-timer in the hospital, a member of the hospital board. In which of these many kinds of status he may be acting depends upon the many subtleties of what is said, by whom, in what context, how, and in what sequence.

As if the interactional picture were not complicated enough, ordinarily two actors may be operating from differently understood status bases. One man may assume that he is a doctor talking to another doctor, while the other is acting as a Negro toward a white. It more often happens, of course, that the interaction is only temporarily "out of joint." Some of the nicer byplays of irony, humor, embarrassment, fright, and the like are traceable to this kind of temporal disjuncture. On the other hand, the course of an interaction is far from unaffected by these misunderstandings, even when they remain unrecognized by one or the other person. My aim here is not so much to underscore the complexity of interaction as to point to some important differences between ordinary everyday interaction and to the vastly simpler sociological model where persons of given status act more or less in a single status at a given time (as nurse to patient).

For the sake of clarity: when only one set of many possible status relationships is thus actualized, let us call what happens "single-structured interaction." By way of extreme contrast, we may suppose that there is very little "structure" in the initial gestures made when two perfect strangers from quite different cultures meet and are uncertain of the appropriate stance to take. When dual or triple bases underlie the course of the interaction (say, female physician and male physician, where both sex and professional status are simultaneously operative), then let us call what happens "multi-structured interaction." Single or multiple, both interactions are conventionally structured because familiar identities are assumed and acted upon.

Since interaction with duration has phases, as well as nuances and unwitting moments, actors must often move from one status base to another during the interplay. For want of a better term we might call this kind of fluid encounter "multi-structured process." Regardless of the terms used, it is important to see that the interaction is, in the sociological sense, "structured"—though the structure of the interaction is more complex than sociologists ordinarily care to consider it.

On the other hand, if we turn to the work of psychiatrists we find that probably they pay more attention to process but understress the structural aspects of interaction. Consider the writings of H. S. Sullivan, with his psychiatric concern for pathologies of interaction. A patient may come into Sullivan's office and instead of acting as patient to psychiatrist, at specific moments he acts toward Sullivan as a particular son to a particular father. It is the psychiatrist's task, Sullivan asserts, to distinguish each phase of interaction from those that precede and succeed it. The pertinence of his observation to our own discussion is that patient-to-psychiatrist is a structured interaction; but son-to-father in this psychiatric interview is so laden with personal experience that it should not be regarded as having quite the same conventional or "cultural" structure. Of course, patient-to-physician relations are also interlarded with personal significances, but for the sake of clarity we would do well to keep the distinction in mind. Sullivan's son (patient)-father (psychiatrist) relationship involves "personal" images. Psychiatrists and psychoanalysts understandably overstress these, and in so doing they are saying, rightly, that people act not merely and always as status representatives. At the same time the social psychologist, I believe, ought to emphasize that interaction is both structured process and interpersonal process.

Psychiatrists touch upon this when they recognize that they themselves act as humanly as does the patient often responding to him personally rather than professionally. But the burden of the psychiatric analysis is in teaching the patient an awareness of the operation and effect of his personal images. The subtleties of the enactment of conventional roles —other than a limited number of them, especially sexual and familial roles—tend to lie outside the range of psychiatric interest. Because psychiatrists have spent their professional lives studying such interaction, their writings have much to say to social psychologists about the interpersonal aspects of interaction. But the social psychologist must work out his own analyses of the more structured—if not necessarily well regulated—modes of intercourse and discourse.

For the study of identity, these modes are crucial. They carry an immense potential for the emergence of new kinds of status and identities. The actors need not be particularly aware or reflective of what is transpiring; having arrived at new phases of relationship, they will eventually invent new concepts to cover a recognition, however vague, that something is new in their world.

Status-Forcing: Its Rules and Strategies

In certain kinds of interaction, the participants know beforehand the several sorts of status that will be represented; and, as in religious rituals, even the exact chronological ordering of action. Very little of human interplay is so predictable and strictly controlled. For most purposes, societies need not assign persons so rigidly their status, nor employ formal mechanisms to make people behave decently and appropriately. We can be relied upon to keep our social places at our own direction and comfort because we learn to be more or less sensitive to interactional cues, and because we apply and obey certain ground rules of interaction.

In the freer, non-ritualistic, forms of interaction we may pass, as I have previously suggested, from one status to another; and this we may do in no fixed, predicted, or regulated order, in fact in no particular order at all. Yet the passage may be governed—even "engineered"—according to conventional understandings and rules, explicit or implicit, of the interactional game. Often the thrusting of another into some status, during the course of an interplay, can have grave consequences both for the interaction itself and for all concerned in it.

Some years ago, Max Sheler, a German philosopher, pointed out that every society possesses means of inducing shame in its members upon proper occasions.[21] What Scheler meant, in our terminology, was that every society—through its agents —can thrust individuals into the status of "shamed one." Each society possesses also the means and power to release individuals from this condition. But we need not confine ourselves to shame alone: groups of every size and composition can, and do, force their members in and out of all kinds of temporary identities. Let us use the term "status-forcing" to designate this process, but extend it to encompass the fact that individuals may force each other into such statuses, without necessarily being clearly or consciously the representatives of specific groups.

A typology, however crude, of such status-forcing will be of illustrative aid. One dimension is the forcing of status "up and down": for instance, to shame, degrade, make a fool or a villain, to heroize, to exalt. A second dimension is forcing the person "in and out" of the group: to exile, excommunicate, hold incommunicado; and all the various steps of approach to the heart or inner sanctum of a group as we see them spelled out, say, in political and religious sects.

Such dimensions as in-out and up-down are but rough and ready ways for indicating the very different bases by which status is assigned; terms such as "shamed" or "degraded" merely point to general and rather vague classes of action. Hence, the meanings and kinds of shame appear to be different to the Japanese than to Westerners. The terms for status actually refer to somewhat different kinds of placement in different social worlds, however similar are the terms themselves. They may also be conceived, perhaps, as continua, as when law courts assign degrees of guilt. The trials of brainwashed Marines, following the Korean War, brought

vividly to public attention some of the anguish associated
with assigning degrees of traitorous status.

There are social rules pertaining to the communicative
processes that render this kind of status placement possible.
To begin with, the conversational context itself is governed,
as Erving Goffman[22] has shown. Although they vary by social
milieu, there are rules for how a conversation gets underway,
how it closes, how people may interrupt without disturbing
the conversation, what they must do to legitimately hold the
center of attention, how others are forced to await their
turn to speak, how the conversationalists can withdraw grace-
fully from the interaction or enter one already in progress.
Likewise there are conventions for forcing persons into, or
for making them accept innumerable positions, however
temporarily.

The rhetorical means of such placement must vary greatly
by the kind of status assignment. Harold Garfinkel has suggested in general terms the formula for forcing public degradation upon a person:

1. Both event and perpetrators must be removed from the
realm of their everyday character and be made to stand as out
of the ordinary. . . .
2. The denouncer must so identify himself to the witnesses
that during the denunciation they regard him not as a private
but as a publicly known person. . . .
3. The denouncer must make the dignity of the supra personal
values . . . salient and accessible to view, and his denunciation
must be delivered in their name.
4. The denouncer must arrange to be invested with the right
to speak in the name of these ultimate values. . . .
5. The denouncer must get himself so defined by the witnesses
that they locate him as a supporter of these values. . . .
6. . . . the denounced person must be ritually separated from
a place in the legitimate order, i.e., he must be defined as standing at a place, 'outside,' he must be made 'strange.'[23]

Orrin Klapp has suggested the different conditions that determine how a person can become a fool and remain one:

Because fool-making is a collective imputation it is not necessary, however, that a person actually have the traits or perform the role of the fool. A person is a fool when he is socially defined. . . . What makes a fool role stick? Among the factors responsible for permanent characterization as a fool we may particularly note (1) repeated performances or obvious personal traits which continually suggest the role of a fool; (2) a striking, conclusive, or colorful single exhibition which convinces the public that the person is irremediably a fool; (3) a story or epithet so 'good' that it is continually repeated and remembered, making up an imperishable legend; and (4) failure to contradict a fool role by roles or stories of a different category.[24]

The rules for forcing status between persons of similar or dissimilar social ranks undoubtedly differ. A subordinate, for instance, insults a superior at least a little differently than another of the same rank; and the tactics one would use on a peer will not do for an older person. Some of the ironies of dramatic comedy arise when the audience realizes that a subordinate is insulting in an extraordinary way a superior, without the latter realizing this for he is used to recognizing insult from subordinates only in particular, conventional, ways. Again, some of the awkwardness of unusual interaction occurs when someone steps out of character and acts up or down to the other, thus forcing the other into some odd, often difficult to formulate, status; as when a precocious child converses with an adult in stunningly equal terms; or an adult, unused to children, attempts to speak with a child "on his own level."

One aspect of the rules dealing with status-forcing is that agents or agencies are certified, or certify themselves, to carry out the placement: courts, parents, priests, and lynching mobs come readily to mind. But there is then an interesting potentiality: namely that everyone may sometime receive legitimation to so judge certain other persons. Thus, although it is usually the physician who announces to a person that he is sick (and ought, as Parsons[25] has observed, therefore to adopt the behavior and motivations proper to a sick person) when no physician is available a friend, a family member, even a stranger may make the placement. A Chicago newspaper recently described how a bartender shot a man who had entered the tavern with intent to rob, and having shot him leaned over to ask him whether he was baptized and getting no answer performed the rite then and there. Every status allows as well as requires that such judgments be made. This is where "obligation" comes in, for "is there a doctor in the house?" is a demand upon the doctor in the house to pass a judgment on someone's exact medical status. Likewise, as a good Christian, the bartender must have felt "obligated" to make his victim also a good Christian.

The institutional context of such judgments makes clear that this kind of identification is not merely a matter of one individual acting toward another. Indeed, we ought not to overlook the frequency with which such judgments are made upon entire groups. The Japanese-Americans were removed from the class of citizens with full rights to a class with limited rights when they were removed from California by emergency law during World War II; and the impact upon the identities of these citizens was considerable. Court decisions may likewise directly or indirectly implicate organizations and groups rather than merely single defendants, sometimes with grave consequences for identity, as with the recent Supreme Court decisions on racial school integration.

These institutional judgments or placements, of course, have great force for one cannot with impunity disregard them; but neither can one disregard quasi-institutional assignments such as occur when a singer is raised to great popularity and is lionized by a mass of adolescent admirers. Popular heroes suddenly raised to fame have found to their dismay, as did Lindburgh, that their formless audiences assign mythical attributes and expect further heroic performance.

Of great importance is the relation of self to those significant others who are assigning "me," for it is common-place that the impact upon self varies greatly by whether one can or cannot afford to ignore the placement. We should not make the mistake of assuming that "afford to ignore" is merely a matter of institutional coercion, as our governmental and legal examples might suggest. The significant other may be effective, terribly so, but have very little institutional weight.

The consequence of such status-forcing for personal identity is an exceedingly complicated matter. This much, at least, must be taken into account: to begin with, it makes a difference whether the placement is temporary (banishment), permanent (exile), or of uncertain duration (idolization). It makes a difference whether the placement is reversible or whether it leads fairly automatically to yet another placement (assignment to jail leads regularly to gestures of rejection toward the ex-convict upon his release, driving otherwise fairly innocent persons to genuine criminal status). A person may be prepared for the placement or, in various degrees, unprepared. Transition to the new status may be by stages or it may be more abrupt. The placement may involve only one "statused" person or several, as when ten boys are punished simultaneously for a school prank. Undoubtedly, the impact upon conception of self will vary, too, depending upon whether the assignment is to a status that has only a few members (heroes) or has many members. Some placements involve great alteration of character (traitorous, impure), but others assume that much less drastic change has occurred.

It would be incorrect to assume from my institutional examples that all forcing is entirely a verbal, name-calling, matter. We may force passage by gesture, or lack of gesture, as when a man puts himself out on a limb because he expects us to acknowledge something he said as brilliant but we do not do so. Likewise, we may lay a trap so that an opponent publicly makes a fool of himself or falls openly into temptation; and we may do this without implicating ourselves. As he may not know the origin of his abasement, the character of his responses or his attempts to counter the status assignment, will be different than when he knows its source. Any discussion of counter strategies must necessarily take this into account.

Thus far I have been talking about status-forcing as if it were a deliberate set of operations. But you can be, and continually are, the unwitting agent of such status-forcing. Goffman,[26] in writing of the constant danger of losing and causing loss of face, makes the point that during conversation everybody is "in jeopardy"; because of the rules covering conversation, one is in constant danger of causing or receiving "affront." The wider point at issue is that much more than potential affront and insult seem to be involved. Interaction carries the potential of unwitting as well as witting imputation of countless motives and character—to others and to self. It can be said consequently that the very nature of interaction implies the forcing of status. It is worth remembering that interaction not only puts everyone concerned in danger—actors and audience alike—but equally exposes everybody to transforming experiences that are more positive and creative in implication.

Because status assignment can be so spontaneous and at the time unwitting, tactics develop, often conventional enough, for removing the other from the new status back to where he was before. If the spontaneous assignment was negative, then we must use certain devices, as Goffman suggests, to restore the interactional "equilibrium." We must make peace offerings, compensate, even declare our own possible blame. Assuredly the devices whether universal or specific to one culture—are many and will vary along some of the dimensions of status already discussed.

Likewise there will be complicated tactics for preventing the assignment, to others and self, when we see it "coming up" in interaction—including the very breaking off of the interaction or adequate preparation at critical phases of the interaction. Other devices exist for countering an assignment after it has occurred, or while it is occurring, since the assignment is sometimes not of a single moment but may take place over a span of time.

However, this is again overlooking the more enhancing and pleasurable assignments of status. Having had a hand in moving a man "upward" or "inward," you necessarily must follow with sets of confirming gestures signifying: "I really meant it," "it is really true," "we did not recognize it before but. . . ." Or, if the assigned person, modest or disbelieving, denies the novel assessment you may seek to reaffirm, reassure, and even to replay the drama of the assignment.

Even if you wish to renege upon your assignment, the bystanders may compel you to obey interactional rules, make you play fair, or in other ways counter your disposition to renege. The recipient of an unexpectedly favorable status may also seek to confirm it further. He may elicit further gestures of affirmation quite directly or indirectly by trying out appropriate behavior and thereby receiving approval. The very act of seeking to further confirm, or compel confirmation, may itself move the interaction along into new phases, and may result in the reassessment and reassignment of identities.

Summing up what I have said about the forcing of status: status positions exist not merely to be filled at appropriate times by appropriate persons—as in rituals; but they get assigned according to the witting judgments and often unwitting impulses evoked during interactional encounters. Status-forcing carries an explosive potential for bringing the encounter to a close in a different place than it started—regardless of the devices (such as apology) that exist for restoring participants to previous positions. This is true

also when we are consciously concerned with ending interaction with the same selves as when we entered; and the
interaction must be all the more precarious when one or
more persons intend or need to change their relationships.
Rules govern the interaction, but not entirely the outcomes.

Control over Interaction

There is such a thing as control over interaction. Some
people are good at this most of the time, some none of the
time; but no one can make the course of interactions run
to his liking every time. The matter of control has not been
sufficiently studied, although the empirical techniques of
"staying on top" of conversations and other interactions are
well known. Something of the theoretical complexities of
seizing, assuming, and regaining control after its loss is suggested by Orrin Klapp's too brief analysis of how a man
can escape from the fool role. He writes:

Among the major routes of escape . . . are the following (1)
Avoidance of the imputation by 'taking a joke and laughing it
off' implies that the jibe is ineffectual or inapplicable. (2) A
counter-joke or effective repartee 'turns the tables.' . . . (3)
. . . accceptance of the fool role and its use as a 'ruse' or 'trap'
for a clever victory. . . . (4) Activity, aggressiveness, or 'fight'
may transform a fool into a hero, particularly when he picks a
larger opponent. . . . Finally, by suffering or showing 'human'
traits which arouse sympathy, a person can escape. . . . If perse-
cution occurs under conditions in which the fool can be identified
with a popular cause, so that his sufferings are seen as sacrifices,
conversion to the very powerful role of martyr is possible.[27]

Part of the process of gaining control over interaction is
certainly unwitting, although perhaps not quite in the same
sense that psychiatrists stress. Certain things about a man's
posture, intonation, speech, pace and modes of interaction
unwittingly force others to respond in ways appropriate to

his—at least seemingly—claimed status. Here is a nice example, nice because divorced from implications of the psychiatrist's kind of unconscious intent, though of course this latter enters into much ordinary projection of a self-image.

A former nurse has described . . . some interesting reactions to a forced changing of sex roles. 'Frankie' was brought to the hospital for examination at the age of five, and 'he' was there diagnosed as a genuine female whose clitoris had been previously mistaken for a small penis. In the children's ward, before the examination, Frankie showed a decided preference for the company of little boys. . . . After the child's real sex had been determined, the nurses were instructed to treat Frankie as a little girl: "This didn't sound too difficult—until we tried it. Frankie simply didn't give the right cues. It is amazing how much your response to a child depends on that child's behavior toward you. It was extremely difficult to keep from responding to Frankie's typically little boy behavior in the same way that I responded to other boys in the ward. And to treat Frankie as a girl was jarring out of key. It was something we all had to remind ourselves to do. Yet the doing of it left us all feeling vaguely uneasy as if we had committed an error.[29]

In the end, Frankie, of course, could not succeed in her quite unwitting control of others' responses: the social definition of sex differences proved too strong. Ordinary interaction involves both this unwitting presentation of self and the kind that consists of a person unconsciously making claims that he is worthy of being flattered, protected, honored, loved, wounded, teased, insulted, and so on. When a psychiatrist is trained to understand his own reactions as they are evoked in the psychiatric interview, he is being trained also (in our terminology) to break the patient's potential control of the interaction.

It may be useful to think of this matter of control and loss of control over interaction in relation to cycles of mood and self-conception. Everyone has had the common experience of being highly elated, and hence of spilling over this

elation into a number of conversations. You find yourself
willynilly setting the conversational tone. The question here
is not why the elation disappears or wears off, but how such
high spirits may force others to accept this temporary state
of being. Grief or deep depression also puts others through
an interactional hoop. Viewing cycles in longer span, you
may also find yourself caught in ascending and descending
spirals of identity, relatively unaffected by single interactional sessions that do no more than temporarily interrupt
the spiral. Some psychiatric tasks turn about the handling
of significant and persistently reappearing cycles and spirals,
but it seems likely that the more ordinary, if less drastic,
movements of identity also are related to control and loss
of control over interaction. Other persons do not, cannot,
will not, dare not, break your projected self-image; or if
they attempt to do so, you are temporarily blind to their
effort. (Such cycles of mood are characteristic also of groups,
evolving and disappearing in the course of collective interchange and reaction. Such moods—one kind is often termed
"a state of tension"—temporarily affect interaction between
entire groups or institutional echelons.)[29]

The kind of claim exerted during "cycles" appears somewhat different than when a more structured kind of status
is claimed; as, for instance, what is due you because of your
age, sex, or social class. The discrepancies between such
structured, hence seemingly reasonable, claims and the re-
fusal of others to play up are also part of the stuff of the
changing of identities. If people will not take the claim
seriously, or do not recognize that it is being put forward,
or forget it, then on both sides status-forcing is engendered;
for expectations are in the act of being unfulfilled, and the
act is to that extent endangered. The tactics are not so very
different perhaps, whether high status or low is being ignored.
Here lies the realm of discounting, teasing, feigning, bluster-
ing, "reminding," "forcing it down their throats," as well

as the use of certain kinds of humor, including the ironical, the macabre, the satirical, and the belittling.

Not only is the effort here to deny the person his asserted status, but to assign him another. Since the assignment may not be structured, as is the one claimed, the result is often to drive him into a temporary status, of the kind I have discussed as status-forcing. For instance, if a client pokes fun at or is ironical toward a pharmacist, who makes claims to being a kind of physician, then the former is forcing "fool" or some other such status upon the latter

I have used the term "claims" rather than "expectations," briefly because the latter class of acts is more characteristic of highly structured interaction, especially the ceremonial and the ritualistic. Insofar as you expect others to act appropriately toward yourself, but there exists no firm base of shared understanding about this, then your expectation probably can be more suitably viewed as a claim. In more strictly structured interaction there are mutual expectations, to use the usual (if limited) sociological terminology; in less structured, there are claims and counter claims, claims and denials, claims and acceptances. Strategies often require temporary acceptances of the other's claim and control over your own, in order not to break off interaction, and to succeed in establishing your long range aims.

What crudely appears like hypocrisy—or at least like politeness—usually is an attempt to bide time rather than to cede claims. As many essayists have commented, social relations could scarcely exist without a certain amount of hypocrisy and conventional masking of thought and sentiment. A failure to exhibit politeness may mean that counter claims are being asserted, but it also may mean a poor timing of that assertion. A claim that is appropriate at some point in the conversation is inappropriate, upsetting, or in bad taste in another.

Paradoxically, we may speak also of claims proffered by

the other. A proffered claim must be accepted or rejected; that is, you must project the suggested image or some other one, and behave, and expect others to behave, accordingly. When the status proffered is better than you believe you deserve then, although you recognize that the right is given to you to act in a certain way, you feel also as if you really have no right to that right. Yet this is a feature of the precarious excitement so often attending the exploration of those new statuses that are not so much discovered as forced upon us by others. My speaking of proffered claims is, in this context, but another way of referring to status-forcing, but it is helpful for pointing to this quality of forced or fostered exploration. I shall have more to say of it shortly when discussing "coaching" and "scheduling." Of course much proffering of status has no particular effect upon precipitating a changed sense of identities; but may be important for helping to confirm one that you already have, or are attempting to gain. "Tell that good joke again, you do it so well," is an implicit affirmation, a recognition of a staked claim. It is an open offer to you to take control of the interaction, or at least of its next episode.

This has been a long chapter, covering much ground. I shall not attempt to summarize it beyond reminding you that it was a sociologist's way of viewing interaction, but with the specific aim of focusing upon changes in personal identity rather than upon group structures. On the other hand, I have attempted to take into account certain implications of group membership as they pertain to interaction. It is unlikely that this kind of perspective would be equally useful for the study of institutions and groups *per se;* but I would at least hazard that the developmental aspect upon which I have dwelt is worth exploring as a basic assumption rather than the more usual one of "equilibrium" and its disturbances.

of development is a trap for the unwary and a battleground for some centuries of philosophic contention. Precisely what are the relationships that hold between beginning, middle and end? This is the nub of the argument. A stand must be taken on this issue by anyone who wishes to account for and study changes in self-conception and behavior. There are two conceptions of development that are most commonly held by social psychologists. To those I wish to contrast a third, less usually assumed.

Visualize a path from its beginning to its end. Along this path runners are scattered, some just starting, others nearing the end. The end of the path represents the final goal; and the closer to it the runner, the more "advanced" he is. This is the metaphor underlying one conception of development; people are more or less developed along certain lines or in regard to certain tasks. The observer, who stands outside the race, possesses tools for measuring crudely or precisely the amount of progress. The metaphor assumes fixed goals or norms against which the aspirants' movements can be chartered. The movement may be conceived as a series of stages or as steps along a continuum. Any mother who has matched her child's progress against the Gesell age norms will find that this metaphor has a familiar ring. Like the idea of a ladder, or an ascent to heaven, arrival at the final goal is a resting place beyond which progress is not calculated. Too slow progress or too quick, as well as failure to reach the final norm, usually leads to "trouble."

Consider now another metaphor. We have before us an uncooked egg. We may choose to boil, scramble, or poach it, or make it into a dozen different kinds of omelet. Regardless of the treatment this egg receives, it remains an egg. Some people like their eggs hard, some soft, and some very finicky eaters draw finer specifications. To the extent that any claim is made that "this egg is now cooked," all this can mean is that in more or less degree the egg is finished. Up to the point where it becomes converted into charcoal and is really finished, the cooking of the egg represents a matter merely of degree: no matter how the egg changes in appearance, it is still "essentially" an egg.

Changes in people may be conceptualized in like fashion. Thus a person during his lifetime may seem to change considerably, but the essential person is assumed to be the same; he is after all the same person, albeit he may suffer severe damage in transit. This metaphor underlies much theorizing in social psychology. It is represented by the very familiar conception that the essential core of personality is laid down early in life and that later changes are variants, although complicated ones, on the initial personality organization.

Development, then, is commonly viewed either as attainment, or as sets of variations on basic themes. In either case, you as the observer of the developmental pattern are omniscient; you know the end against which persons are matched, or you know the basic themes on which variations are composed. Neither metaphor captures the open-ended, tentative, exploratory, hypothetical, problematical, devious, changeable, and only partly-unified character of human courses of action. Horace Kallen has put it well:

Personal accounts of progress uncover no single pattern, no straight, inevitable line, developmental or other. They speak of regressions and other shifts of interest or direction; changes of field, of method, and of tempo; of new lives, new careers supervening.[1]

Development (or the relations between "permanence and change," between "before and after") may be conceptualized as a series of related transformations. Etymologically the term "transformation" invites us to consider changes in form—changes in being, kind or psychological status.

An example will illustrate this, and other related points as well. When children begin to learn a classificatory terminology—say, distinctions having to do with numbers or money

—their initial conceptions are crude and inaccurate; but since classifications are always related to other classifications, never standing in isolation, even a very young child's classifications cohere, hang together. As he "advances," his earlier concepts are systematically superseded by increasingly complex ones. The earlier ones are necessary for the later; each advance depends upon the child's understanding a number of prerequisite notions. As the newer classifications are grasped, the old ones become revised or qualified, or even drop out entirely from memory. These changes in conceptual level involve, of course, changes in behavior, since behaving is not separate from classifying. Shifts in concept connote shifts in perceiving, remembering and valuing—in short, radical changes of action and person. Hence a child going through different "stages of knowledge" is not merely acquiring more and more knowledge, but may be viewed as becoming transformed.

In speaking of children's development, a directional terminology of advancement or improvement is almost always used, although it need not be. Leaving aside questions of direction, it is perfectly clear that conceptual change—hence transformation—no less marks the course of adult careers. Utilizing the dual meaning of the word "terms," I am suggesting that in coming to new terms a person becomes something other than he once was. Terminological shifts necessitate, but also signalize, new evaluations: of self and others, of events, acts, and objects; and the transformation of perception is irreversible; once having changed, there is no going back. One can look back, but he can evaluate only from his new status.

Some transformations of identity and perspective are planned, or at least fostered, by institutional representatives; others happen despite, rather than because of, such regulated anticipation; and yet other transformations take place outside the orbits of the more visible social structure, although not necessarily unrelated to membership within them. As a way of introducing these several dimensions of personal change, I shall discuss next certain critical incidents that occur to force a person to recognize that "I am not the same as I was, as I used to be." ("Turns occur in experience when the program is stopped in its tracks and the plan is gone with the wind."[2]) These critical incidents constitute turning points in the onward movement of personal careers.

Turning Points

For our purposes there is not much point in describing in detail what takes place at such turning points beyond noting the frequent occurrence of misalignment—surprise, shock, chagrin, anxiety, tension, bafflement, self-questioning —and also the need to try out the new self, to explore and validate the new and often exciting or fearful conceptions. Rather than discussing critical junctures in general, let us consider their typology. The list will not be a long one, but long enough to suggest the value both of its extension and of relating turning points to changes of identity.

A change in your relations with others is often so mundane, so gradual that it passes virtually unnoticed. Some incident is needed to bring home to you the extent of the shift. A marker of progression, or retrogression, is needed. When the incident occurs it is likely to strike with great impact, for it tells you: "Look! you have come way out to here! This is a milestone!" Recognition then necessitates new stances, new alignments. A striking example of the "milestone" is found in the autobiographies of many immigrants to America who later visited their native lands, only then realizing how little affinity they had retained, how identified they had become with America and Americans. Any return home, insofar as you have really left it, will signalize some sort of movement in identity. Some people literally go back home in an effort both to deny how far they have strayed and to prevent further defection.

Sometimes the path of development is foretold but is not believed, either because he who forecasts is distrusted or because his prophecy cannot be understood. Prophets not only point out new directions: they give you measuring rods for calculating movement if you happen to traverse the paths prophesized. This is certainly one of the critical experiences in the psychology of conversion. For instance, a recruit to a religious sect, only partly convinced, is told what will happen when he tries to explain his new position to his old minister, attempts to sell pamphlets to the heathen, and so on, and lo! events turn out as predicted. The prediction will be in terms of a new vocabulary, hence when the vocabulary is shown to be workable the recruit is well on the road toward adopting it in part or *in toto*. The point holds for any kind of conversion—occupational, political, or what not. A novice is told by the old-timer, "Your clients will be of such and such sorts and you'll have such and such experiences with them." When the graph of experience is thus plotted and confirmed, then the person can recognize his own transformation.

Forecasting is often institutionalized in such a fashion that public proclamation is made: "Said candidate has followed the predicted and prescribed path of experience and has gotten to the desired point. Kneel, knight, and receive knighthood. Come to the platform and receive your diploma." When paths are institutionalized, a candidate can easily mark his progress, note how far he has come, and how far he has yet to go. If there are the usual institutionalized acknowledgments of partial steps toward the goal, then these may constitute turning points in self-conception also. If the institutionalized steps are purely formalized, are no longer invested with meaning by the institution, or if the candidate believes them of no real significance, they will not, of course, be turning points for him.

Private proclamation to a public audience is quite another matter. Having announced or avowed your position, it is not easy to beat a retreat. Often you find yourself in interpersonal situations climbing out on a limb, announcing a position, and then having to live up to it. In a more subtle sense, one often marks a recognition of self-change by announcement, but this announcement itself forces a stance facing forward since the way back, however tempting it may still look, is now blocked.

A related turning point—since ceremonial announcement often follows it—is the meeting of a challenge, either self-imposed or imposed by others. Any institution, for instance, possesses regularized means for testing and challenging its members. If you are closely identified with the institution, some tests will be crucial for your self-regard. If you pass them, everyone recognizes that you have met the challenge. However, some challenges, although they occur in institutional settings, are not themselves institutionalized. For instance every student nurse early in her training must face the situation of having a patient die in her arms. For some nurses this appears to be a turning point for self-conception: the test is passed and she—in her own eyes at least—has new status; she can now think of herself as more of a professional. Crucial tests are imposed by individuals on themselves; if they pass they have been psychologically baptized, so to speak, but if they fail then a new path must be taken, a new set of plans drawn up. Naturally, failure does not always result in immediate self-transformation, but may lead to more complete preparation until the test is definitely failed or passed.

One potent form of self-test is the deliberate courting of temptation. Failure to resist it is usually followed by new tests or by yielding altogether. The fuller meaning of temptation is this: you are withdrawing from an old psychological status and coming into a new, and in doing so something akin to the "withdrawal symptoms" of drug addiction occurs. When you are able to resist temptation then an advance is signalized; but when no longer even tempted, you are well aware of having progressed still further. Institutions find it easier to check upon the overt resistance of their members than upon their covert desires. Genuine conversion means the death of old desires. "Backsliding" signifies a failure to resist temptation; frequent backsliding results in a return to previous status or change to yet another.

A rather subtle type of transforming incident occurs when you have played a strange but important role and unexpectedly handled it well. Whether you had considered this an admirable or a despicable role does not matter. The point is that you never thought you could play it, never thought this potential "me" was in yourself. Unless you can discount your acts as "not me" or as motivated by something not under your control, you bear the responsibility or the credit for the performance. Cowardly and heroic roles are both likely to bring unexpected realignment in self-regard. But more usual, and more subtle, are those instances where you find yourself miraculously able to enact roles that you believed—at least as yet—beyond you. Every person new to a job finds himself, through no fault of his own, at some point taken by clients or fellow workers as of more advanced status than he is. This is akin to a light colored Negro "passing" unwittingly as a white. Once having carried off the disguise, you realize something new about yourself. The net result is likely to be that you wish to experiment with this new aspect of yourself. Conversely, there are roles previously viewed with suspicion, even despised, that you now find yourself enacting with unexpected success and pleasure. You must either wash your hands of it, actually or symbolically—

as in *Macbeth*—or came to grips with this new aspect of yourself.

It is probable that some of the effect of experimental role-dramas is that the drama allows and forces the person to play a range of roles he did not believe himself capable of playing, or never conceived of playing; it brings him face to face with his potential as well as his actual self. Sociable parties, Robert Potter has suggested, by their very episodic and expressive nature, allow and further such exploration of roles.[3] Similarly, some of the effect of psychiatric therapy seems to rest upon the skill of the psychiatrist in making the patient face up to the full range of his acts, rather than repress awareness of them or blame them upon outside forces.

A critical experience with built-in ambivalence occurs when someone surpasses the performance of another after whom he had formerly patterned himself, as when a student overtakes his beloved teacher, or a son exceeds his father's social position. When allegiance is very strong this awareness of overtaking the model may be crippling, and refuge is sought by drawing back from the abyss of departure. To be a success, one must surpass his models and depart from them. Departures are institutionalized in America by such mechanisms as myths of success, by the easy accessibility of higher social positions, and by the blessings of parents who in turn experience vicarious success through the performances of their offspring. Despite the institutionalized devices for reducing the strain of upward departure, ambivalence and stress undoubtedly persist even for many of our most successful climbers.

Another kind of transforming experience, one with shattering or sapping impact, is betrayal—by your heroes, in fact by anybody with whom you are closely "identified." Betrayal implicates you as well as him, in exceedingly subtle ways. Consider three varieties. When you have closely pat-

terned yourself after a model, you have in effect "internalized" what you suppose are his values and motives. If the
model abandons these, he leaves you with a grievous dilemma. Has he gone over to the enemy?—then you may with
wry smile redouble your efforts along the path he laid out
when he was still pure. Or did he lead you up an illusory
path of values?—then with cynicism and self-hate you had
better abandon your former self too. A different species of
betrayal, involving search for atonement, is illustrated by
the stunned American mother whose son, a captured prisoner
of the Chinese Communists, became converted to Com-
munism and refused to return to America. The cry here
is always: "Where did I go wrong that he, an extension of
me, should go wrong?" A third variety of betrayal often goes
by the name of "rejection"; that is, rejection of you after
you had closely identified with him. Here the beloved has
symbolically announced that you and your values are not
right, or at least are not wholly satisfying. Second-generation
rejection and drift away from immigrant parents illustrates
this. Betrayal of this type consists, usually, of a series of
incidents, rather than of a single traumatic event. During
the course of day-to-day living, decisions are made whose
full implications are not immediately apparent. People can
go on deceiving themselves about paths that actually have
been closed by those decisions. At the point when it becomes apparent that former possibilities are dead issues,
the person stands at a crossroads. A severe instance of such
a turning point occurs when someone traps himself into an
occupation—much as a house painter might paint himself
unthinkingly into a corner of the room—believing that he
can always get out when he wants to. The jazz musician who
goes commercial "just for a while" to make money, may
find eventually that the commercial style has caught him,
that he can no longer play real jazz as it should be played.
This kind of crossroad may not be traumatic, but nostalgi-

cally reminiscent, signifying then that the gratifications arising from past decisions are quite sufficient to make past
possibilities only pleasantly lingering "maybes." Final recognition that they are really dead issues is then more of a
ritualistic burial and is often manifested by a revisiting of
old haunts—actually or symbolically.

A final type of critical experience that I shall discuss is
akin to betrayal, but the agent of destruction is less personal.
A man may realize that he has been deceived, not by any
specific person but by events in general. If the deception
strikes home severely, he may respond with self-hate, "Why
did I not discover this before?"; with personalized resentment against someone "Why did they not tell me?"; or with
diffuse resentment against the world in general. An essential
aspect of this critical experience is that a man's naming of
self is disoriented. He is not what he thought he was. Self-
classificatory disorientation, of course, can be mild. For
instance, a Jewish boy, brought up in a moderately Orthodox
home, discovered later that all Jews were not Orthodox,
but that there were Reformed Jews (who made him feel
not at all Jewish) and very Orthodox Jews (who made him
feel not at all Jewish). Such discoveries come as shocks, but
not necessarily as traumas. There is more anguish involved
when a person finds that although he believed he possessed a
comfortable dual identity, Negro and American, significant
others are now challenging one of those identities. This is,
or at least was, an unnerving experience for many Northern
Negroes who visited in the South, however much they may
have read or been warned. This negation of a portion of
identity may not provide much of a crisis if the person with-
draws from his attackers, but if he stays, as some Negroes
have stayed in the South, he must make his peace with the
challenging audience. A more crucial juncture in the maintenance of identity occurs when a person discovers that one
of his chief self-referential terms is completely erroneous.

Cases in point are adopted children who do not discover
until later years the fact of their adoption, and those occasional tragic cases of children who are raised as members
of the opposite sex and eventually discover the mis-naming.
Imagine also the destructive effects, compounded with guilt
and self-hate, of discovering an actual identity with a group
formerly reviled and despised, as for instance an anti-Semite
discovering that he is partly Jewish.

Enough has been said about various types of turning
points to suggest that these are points in development when
an individual has to take stock, to re-evaluate, revise, resee,
and rejudge. Although stock-taking goes on within the single
individual, it is obviously both a socialized and a socializing
process. Moreover, the same kinds of incidents that precipi-
tate the revision of identity are extremely likely to befall
and to be equally significant to other persons of the same
generation, occupation, and social class. This is equivalent
to saying that insofar as experiences and interpretations
are socially patterned, so also will be the development of
personal identities. Let us look next at some types of social
patterning; those associated with regulated movements of
persons into and from social positions in organized groups.
This will enable us to place turning points into close conjunction with formal organizations; yet will not commit
us to the position that changes of identity are invariably
associated with social position in formal organizations.

Regularized Status-Passage[4]

Membership in any enduring group or social structure
inevitably involves passage from status to status. In order that
a group persist and flourish, each status must be filled, jobs
must be done. The incumbents of positions die, retire, leave,
fail, and sometimes betray the organization. New kinds of

goals develop and so new positions are created. Other positions get sloughed off, and persons who previously filled them must shift or be shifted elsewhere. Lengthy retention in a given status may hide a genuine shift of social position, as old duties and prerogatives are dropped and new ones accrue. Unless a group were to be wholly undifferentiated, its members necessarily have to move up, down, and sideways.

Many passages of status are highly institutionalized, so that individuals move through them in orderly sequence. Professorial ranks in colleges and universities are an instance of such a step-by-step progression; but so is the normal movement from bride to wife to pregnant mother to rearer of children. When movement is thus regularized, this means that there are predecessors and successors: people have been there before and will follow you. This gives continuity not only to the group or organization, but also to personal experience. In a host of ways, you are prepared for what is to come, are made aware of the immediacy of the next transition, are reminded that you have just now made a passage. The attainment of status may require that you have certain experience, and meet certain standards of conduct and performance; these, myth and story, example and direct instruction, are indispensable. The more subtle aspects of preparation include forewarning you that certain things will soon happen, that you will experience certain experiences, and feel certain feelings; and when you do, certain predecessors will stand ready with interpretations of such predicted events. Their interpretations embody the special language of the group. *Post facto* explanations are also at hand, so that when a person encounters situations for which he has no definitions, he will be offered ready-made ones. "We all went through this." "At your age, that happened to me too. It means that. . . ."

Providing that the definitions offered are not too many

and too divergent, you are thereby moved along an orderly line of development. By organizing your action in terms of preferred rationale, you thereby confirm their usefulness and validity. I say validity because your action then can be easily named by other people, and familiarly even comfortably responded to. Merton in another connection has called this the "self-fulfilling prophesy"[5]—although I am emphasizing here primarily the continuity that an acceptance of rationale affords. Thus, advice given within an occupation to incoming personnel about clients serves to perpetuate certain relationships and experiences with the clients.

If conflicting rationales leave a person in definitional confusion, or if for other reasons he reaches novel interpretations of his experience, the regulated chain of status-progression is threatened. However, alternative explanations of given events may traditionally exist within a single institution, so that the acceptance by a novice of one or another explanation sets immediate conditions for the pursuit of alternative career routes. This, indeed, is true not merely at the inception of a career but at any point along it, providing that unexpected situations and experiences are traditionally rationalized. Thus a young professor who discovers that he has neither the ability nor the incentive for genuinely excellent research, can find institutional sanction and rationale for devoting himself to building a reputation as an outstanding teacher of undergraduates.

When positional mobility follows known sequences, different motivations frequently become appropriate at each successive status. Passage from one to another involves not only changes of action and demeanor, but of the verbalized reasons that are associated with them. Indeed, the stability of a given social structure rests largely upon a proper preparation for these sequential steps. Motivations appropriate to earlier—and usually lower—status must be sloughed off or transmuted, and new ones added or substituted. This necessity is marvelously illustrated in a description by Arensberg and Kimball of family transition in Irish peasant families.[6] At the time of the son's marriage, a series of cognate changes in status, act, and motivation are intended to occur simultaneously. The father must yield control of family policy and cease active work; the son must assume responsibility and ardently wish to do so; the mother must become a household guide and teacher to her son's wife; and the latter must remain temporarily subservient. But the younger woman must also be properly motivated to leave her own family, physically and psychologically, and to become a mother as quickly as possible. When her child is born, the young mother must enthusiastically assume full household responsibility. Simultaneous with this momentous event, the old couple pass to a status of old age. This latter change carries with it an organization of perspective and activity that can be called "making ready for death," the next—and last—status. At any step of this complicated drama of progression, things will go awry if the actors lag behind or speed up unduly in their action or rationale. And, in fact, the strains in family and community life fall exactly at those points where the speed of transition gets out of alignment.

Even in relatively stable structures, where career paths are regular and well regulated, there always arise problems of pacing and timing. Ideally speaking, successors and predecessors should move in and out of offices at equal speeds, but they do not and cannot. Persons who are asked to move may be willing to do so, but must make actual and symbolic preparation to leave. Meanwhile, a successor may be waiting impatiently to take over. In status-passage, transition periods are a necessity for people often invest heavily of themselves in a position, come to possess it as it possesses them, and it is no easy matter for them to sever themselves from it. If the full ritual of leave-taking is not allowed, a person may be for some time only partially in his new status. On the other hand the institution stands ready with devices to make him forget, to plunge him into the new office, to point out and allow him to experience the gratifications accruing to it, as well as to force him to abandon the old. Where statuses pyramid so that each is conceived as the logical and temporal extension of the last, severance is not such a disturbing experience. But even here if a person must face his old associates in unaccustomed roles, problems of loyalty become knotty. For this reason, a period of tolerance immediately after formal admission to the new status is almost a necessity. This tolerance is rationalized with phrases like "it takes time," "he is not quite yet in it," "we all make mistakes when starting, until we learn that. . . ."

But people not only drag their heels, they may be too zealous, too eager. Those who are new to a position often commit the indelicate error of taking formal promotion or certification much too literally, when actually there exist intervening informal stages that must be traversed before the full prerogatives of position are attained. This passage may involve tests of loyalty as well as the simple accumulation of information and skill. These informal status grades are referred to in the special language of rankings: "he's a *new* lieutenant" or "that board member is one of the old-timers." An overeager person may be kept in line by all kinds of controlling devices; for instance, a new sales manager discovers that it will take "just a little while" before things can be arranged so that the can institute the changes he envisages in his department. Even a newly appointed superior has to face the resentments or cautiousness of personnel who have preceded him in the organization; and he may, if sensitive, pace his "moving in on them" until he has passed unspoken tests.

When a man is raised to the rank of his former superiors, an especially delicate situation is created. Officially he is now equal to, or like, his former teachers and elders. But equality is neither created by that official act nor, even if it were, could it come about without a certain awkwardness. Imagery and patterns of responses must be rearranged on both sides, and strong self-control must be exerted in order that acts be kept appropriate—even to the self-conscious use of first names, often violating an outmoded but still strongly operative sense of propriety. Slips are inevitable, for although the new status may be fully granted proper situational identities may be temporarily forgotten to everyone's embarrassment. The former subordinate may come eventually to command, or take precedence over, someone toward whom he previously looked for guidance. At the very least, the colleagues may have to oppose each other over some crucial issue which arises and divides people of the same rank. When former sponsors and sponsored now find it necessary to array themselves differently on such issues, recrimination becomes overt and betrayal explicit. It is understandable why men who have been promoted often prefer to take office, or are advised to do so, in another agency or organization or branch office, however great their desire for remaining at home.

The problems attending the speed of status-passage are merely part of the larger organizational problem of recruiting members for various posts. Recruitment is generally thought of only in connection with bringing newcomers into the structure; but insofar as replacements must be found for each position, on every level, personnel either must be brought in from the outside or trained in other internal positions. In both cases, persons must be induced to give up current endeavors and commitments in order to move onward and, usually, upward. Within the organization, certain persons must be deterred from aiming too high, but others must be induced to cease practicing prized skills and to give up clear satisfactions in exchange for the presumed rewards of the next position. If the latter rewards seem great enough, candidates for each position will be found; but if they are improperly motivated to move to the new position, they will experience considerable strain in transit. Until engineers became used to the idea that their careers frequently involved beginning as engineers and ending as administrators, they experienced severe shocks to personal identity when as administrators they ceased practicing their engineering skills. E. C. Hughes has recounted the story of one engineer who dreamed a nightmare, in which he had lost the capacity to operate a slide rule.[7] In social science research nowadays, it has become necessary for some research professors to spend time and energy finding research money for their junior colleagues. "I spend my time on this. I'm always working on it, I spend my evenings writing letters, seeing people, telephoning. I have to make sacrifices in my own research, of course."[8] The Harvard professor from whom this quote is taken must be ready and willing to append "of course" to his sacrifice of research and its satisfactions—otherwise his personal dissatisfactions will outweigh the benefits, accruing to his juniors and to the department, of his contribution toward the common organizational task of raising necessary funds.

Indeed, at every level of an organization, personal stress can arise if motivations are inappropriate for further passages. Self-conceptions may mesh with or grate against institutional arrangements for sequential movements. At Harvard University, few assistant professors can expect to attain the tenure ranks; most anticipate going to other colleges and universities after a maximum of five years. If an assistant professor regards his years at Harvard as stimulating and prestigeful preparation for a better post elsewhere, he is relieved of many strains of competition. But he must guard himself—and some do so insufficiently— against putting down roots into the community and prevent himself from hoping, however vaguely, that he will be extended tenure. Harvard is able to recruit its assistant professors so effectively—from its own graduate schools as well as from other universities—only because this rank is an early step of career that is completed elsewhere.

When occupancy of a status is accompanied by acute strain, there is an enhanced possibility that the regular or institutionalized sequence of steps will be abandoned. At these points, people break away in desperation or with defiance, and leave occupations, families, social classes and other such organizing frameworks of commitment and loyalty. If recruits are plentiful and not too much time, effort, and money have been expended upon them, their loss may be regarded as minimal. Otherwise steps must be taken to prevent such defection. The conditions that are causing personal stress must be examined, greater rewards offered, in order that stress can better be endured; and alternative career paths must be opened up, or at least seem to aspirants to have opened up. However, the occurrence of stressful situations may not force a man entirely out but merely lead him to aim at a different career within the organization or establishment; causing him to abandon the greater effort necessary to reach the top ranks or to shift his aspirations to other channels. Some choices of specialty and vocation involve this kind of shifting as when one abandons a line of occupational endeavor but uses it or its skills to make the shift. Hence in certain specialties, until the routes of entry become institutionalized, recruits are drawn from many fields, often from their failures or their rebellious members. This means that these men are embarked upon an uncertain though not necessarily hazardous future, since the sequences of status-passage have not yet been precisely laid down and sanctified by tradition.

When organizations and institutions are expanding, forming, disintegrating, or in any way changing radically, the personal lives of their members are rendered more tortuous and uncertain and at the same time more dangerous and more exciting. The opportunities for power and personal advance in expanding social structures are obvious, but even when the latter are disintegrating, some clever or fortunate people forge new career opportunities. The dangers of rapid organizational change—whether of expansion or contraction—can be illustrated by what happens to old-timers who reach high positions only to find these no longer carry distinctive prerogatives and honors. Danger also dogs the novice who blindly follows old career models, for a model always is in some significant regard out of date, unless the times and the institutions are relatively stable. During such periods of great institutional change, the complexities of career are further compounded by what is happening to the careers of those others with whom one is significantly involved. The ordinary ties of sponsorship weaken and break because those in positions to sponsor are focused upon matters more immediately germane to their own careers. The lower ranks feel the consequences of unusual pressures generated among the ranks above. People become peculiarly vulnerable to unaccustomed demands for loyalty and alliance which spring from unforeseen organizational changes.

Insofar as careers can be visualized and implemented because of the relative stabilities of those social structures within which one has membership, the continuity and maintenance of identity is safeguarded and maximized, and methods of maintenance and restoration are more readily utilized and evolved. However, the movement from status to status, as well as the frustration of having to remain unwillingly in a status, sets conditions for the change and development of identities. Although my examples have been chosen mainly from work organizations, this way of looking at adult development is not at all restricted to occupational life. The lives of men and women can—theoretically at least—be traced as a series of passages of status. Insofar as this is so, we most heartily agree with Erikson's striking statement that a sense of identity "is never gained nor maintained once and for all. Like a good conscience, it is constantly lost and regained. . . ."[9]

Coaching

When passages of status are more or less well regulated, those who have gone through the recognized steps stand ready, as I have said, to guide and advise their successors. This guidance is essential, for even regulated passage is perhaps more hazardous than my account has indicated.

In the well known novel, *The Late George Apley,* J. P. Marquand[10] portrays the well ordered life of George as it follows the traditional Bostonian upper class pattern of growing up and growing old. As a young man, George is in danger of being drawn off the track, when he becomes fond of an Irish girl far below him in social position. He is brought to heel through family pressure and by being shown how this incident "really" fits into his entire expected life cycle. Natural as it is for him to dally with such a girl, the "escapade" is not to be treated as a serious venture. The great danger of such an escapade is that through it some George Apley—if not this one—will be drawn off expected paths and lost to family and social class. However, the counsel of elders is requisite to status passages for reasons other than hazard, since all the future steps are clear only to those who have traversed them. Certain aspects of what lies over the horizon are blurred to the candidate, no matter how clear may be his general path. This forces his predecessors not only to counsel and guide him, but to prepare and coach him beforehand. Coaching is an integral part of teaching the inexperienced—of any age.

Once we see this function of "the coach," we are prepared to discuss coaching quite apart from regularized status steps, and within wider contexts than athletics or professional drama. A coaching relationship exists if someone seeks to move someone else along a series of steps, when those steps are not entirely institutionalized and invariant, and when the learner is not entirely clear about their sequences (although the coach is). The football coach attempting to turn out a good half-back, Iago seeking to induce Othello along the path of jealousy, the piano teacher trying to make a concert pianist out of a young man, the revivalist trying to work his audience into a frenzy of conversion, the psychiatrist carefully maneuvering his patient back to better psychological integration, and the confidence man manipulating his victim through sequential steps of involvement in an illicit deal: all are instances of coaching relationships, albeit each has different aspects. In each instance there is a man who has yielded himself (whether he knows it or not) to a teacher who guides him along at least partly obscure channels. Since every field in which such teaching goes on has its own prescriptions and rules of thumb, my discussion of coaching quite obviously must be very general, and will be pointed particularly toward those changes of identity that take place during coaching.

The general features of the coaching relationship flow from the learner's need for guidance as he moves along, step by step. He needs guidance not merely because in the conventional sense he needs someone to teach him skills, but because some very surprising things are happening to him that require explanation. The coach stands ready to interpret his responses, which may otherwise only have the status of ambiguous signs. If you look at something as nonpsychological as learning a physical skill, perhaps you can see the point more easily. The learner leans upon the coach's expert advice, for instance, whether a given muscular movement is going to lead forward, or down a false path; and without the coach he may not even notice his own movement. The coach literally calls attention to new responses: "Look, this is the first time you have managed to do this." Likewise, the coach explains away responses, saying "pay no attention" for what is happening either should be regarded as of no importance or as something that happens only "at this stage." The next steps are pointed out ("Don't worry, wait, this will happen"). In sum: because the sequences of steps are in some measure obscure, and because one's own responses become something out of the ordinary, someone must stand prepared to predict, indicate, and explain the signs.

But the tutor generally assigns himself a far more active role than I have suggested. He does not merely wait for the student to develop new responses; he throws him into situations so as to elicit certain responses from him. This provides an opportunity to indicate, interpret, and predict. Understandably, this involves the coach in a certain kind of duplicity upon occasion (as when a fencing teacher allows his pupil to hit him for the first time); the coach's position also requires that he may have to function like a playwright, arranging episodes, setting scenes, getting supporting characters to act in a certain way. Of course the pupil, by virtue of his acquisition of new skills or new perspectives, can be counted upon to engage other persons in new interactions. Like the infant who upon learning his first words encounters his parents differently, the learner's recently gained skills will throw him into novel situations. Some outcomes will be gratifying, but of course others can be terrifying or at least frightening. The coach utilizes both kinds of outcomes to retain control, occasionally even allowing him his head so as to be able to say—"I told you so, now then you see. . . ." The point is that the untutored can not see until he has tried for himself, just as generally he cannot visualize much of the proper path beforehand.

In malevolent kinds of coaching—as in seduction, or in conning by confidence men—the relationship is one of trapper and victim. However, in almost all coaching there appears to be a strong element of inducement, temptation, and behind-the-scenes action. The con man baits, tempts, induces; but so does, although in less obvious ways, the art teacher, the basketball coach, or the psychiatrist. Abstractly stated, the coach not only works on current desires to get action directed along given paths, but seeks to create new desires and aims. He seeks to create a new identity for the pupil—or the victim—and to do this involves him in a variety of canny maneuvers.

In general, we should be struck by the importance of timing in all coaching. Because the pupil is being guided in his moves—muscularly, psychologically, socially—the coach is preoccupied with teaching him certain things at correct places and times. To begin with, the coach may be rejected if he forces too fast a pace, especially at the outset. The pupil may lose face or become frightened or otherwise distressed. In psychiatric coaching the patient may go elsewhere for help or, if the relationship is involuntary as when he is committed to a mental hospital, simply withdraw psychologically. On the other hand, the pupil (whether a patient, victim, or convert) may be lost to his mentor if the latter moves too slowly—lost through boredom, shattering of faith, or other reasons. Of course, the teacher may call attention to his superior experience and wisdom, as well as draw upon the resources of trust placed in him by the other, in order to set the pace; but he does so always at some risk. This risk is unavoidable and can only be minimized by shrewd tactics. The coach has to know when to force his man over a

hurdle, and when to let him sidle up to it; when to schedule definite moves, and when to allow a period of relative
free play. The coach must skillfully balance between two
poles: he must not pressure the student by his own impa-
tience; yet he must force movement at those junctures when
the fellow appears ready but reluctant to move, is in fact
really "there" but does not realize it.

Crucial tactics in this delicately balanced process are the
prescription, the schedule, the challenge, the trial, and the
accusation. Prescriptions for action are sometimes called
"routines" or "exercises" or "lessons"; they are traditional
step-by-step progressions that prepare the way for further
movement. When the coaching relationship is well-institu-
tionalized, such routine practices become a very visible and
sometimes hampering part of the coaching profession. The
schedule is also an integral aspect of the coaching process;
notions arise of how fast or how slowly the pupil should
move, and at what points he should move slower or faster.
There is at least an implicit set of norms governing how
quickly he should progress through certain stages. Recently,
a psychologist has suggested to a group of psychiatrists how
a standardized set of norms might be used to measure the
progress of their patients. In the coaching relationship, a
considerable potential strain exists because the coach must
control his own impulses to standardize schedules too greatly.

Challenges or dares are also an invariant aspect of coaching. Since a person is being asked to relinquish old modes
of doing and seeing, he is in effect being asked to do and
say and even think things that look risky or dangerous. I
recently heard a psychiatrist say to a patient, "It is now
time to do. . . . You may fail but you are likely not to; it
is a risk worth taking." Of course, there are clever and institutionalized ways of cushioning failure, but the important
thing is that the person by meeting the challenge receives an

indication of how far he has progressed. His overcoming of
a challenge provides a marker, a milestone of his development.

Essential also to coaching is the accusation, hurled or
insinuated. The coach will conceive of his pupil on occasion
as backsliding, as giving in to old habits, old temptations,
and therefore must be frankly reprimanded. The pupil will
also be accused of loss of faith or trust: "How can you bene-
fit from what I have to teach you if you do not trust me
now." From the learner's perspective, the coach may be
neglecting his job, ruining one's talents, breaking faith, even
engaging in betrayal. Accusations both block the process of
learning and are vitally important for those reconciliations
that mark turning points on the road forward.

I have mentioned the elements of risk and trust involved
in the coaching relationship, although they loom as more
obvious in some kinds of relationships than in others. The
novice airplane pilot literally puts his life at the disposal
of his instructor. In seduction or in confidence games the
secret motivations that are involved highlight the risk and
danger. Even in such mundane pursuits as piano and voice
teaching or training for track meets, the pupil's potential
level of performance may be greatly endangered by im-
proper counsel. Insofar as the coaching process also leads
to great changes of identity—as in G. B. Shaw's apocraphal
drama *Pygmalion*—you, as a pupil, are in large measure
ceding an unknown destiny to a mentor who presumably
knows where he is taking you. A special danger is that the
relationship may be broken off midstream, before "the
treatment" is completed, with potential danger to both but
particularly to the learner. One of the great, and inevitable
risks of coaching is precisely that the coach may die, or
move away, leaving the student vulnerable in various ways:
because he is in a stage of self-imputed personal helpless-
ness, or standing upon the brink of a learning crisis, or not

yet properly out of love with the coach ("transference"), or in the midst of meeting a great challenge. But a comparable risk is that the student has the final responsibility of judging when the coaching relationship is genuinely harmful to himself or to his "potential." There is a point beyond which he must not, like Cinderella, stay. The coach may have poor judgment. It is not impossible even that he evinces faulty judgment because he loves or hates his pupil too much; although he may be actually malevolent or merely indifferent. The learner always has an obligation to himself of assessing when he is being harmed and when he is being helped, even in those very traditional situations where the coach is supposed supremely knowledgable.

The reverse side of great risk and danger is trust and faith. To this should be added what the psychoanalysts call "identification"; that is, a very close modeling of self after the other, or after certain of his aspects. The coach is not only a partial model ("do as I do"), but in certain stages may become almost a total model ("be as I am" or "wish to be what I am"). The tutor, of course, may consciously utilize this desire or propensity. On the other hand, in many types of coaching, particularly after the earlier stages of learning, mere imitation is not sufficient for progress.

Let us now consider more explicitly the shifts of identity brought about through coaching, as against the mere acquisition of skill. One cannot, of course, discuss risk, trust, identification, duplicity, challenge, and merely talk of the acquisition of skill. In some coaching, the person may be taken as a *tabula rasa,* as if he had no previous commitments of the kind the coach is now about to build; the task is simply to build upon unimpeded ground. More often this is not a realistic stance for the coach to take. The learner has something to unlearn, to cope with, and this will enter the trajectory of his learning early and often stay with him until very late. This is perhaps another way of saying that the coach must challenge old modes of doing, seeing, and thinking, as well as point out new modes. When the learning and re-learning is extreme—and I shall consider a variety of this in the next section—there must be massive and frontal attack upon identities. In less drastic kinds of change, through the agency of coaches, a man is requested also to turn his back upon his past, to discount previous accomplishments, to divest himself of earlier prides, to disidentify himself with old practices, old allies, and even old loves.

One may sometimes observe during the initial sessions of a new coaching relationship how the participants gingerly hold back from much involvement until they are "sure." This is especially true of the student, but the teacher also may have provisos. Traditionally, the early phases may be coached in terms of "make-believe" or "not for keeps"; and institutionally they may take the form of not yet counting the score or recording the performance. All this, in a sense, represents a trial period; one is involved, but without much commitment to his own performance, and can retreat with honor and dignity. It is as if there were a kind of moratorium, during which effort is great but during which both sides ceremonially ignore negative performances. Of course, such a moratorium and such make-believe run all through the coaching process, perhaps particularly during the new phases in cycles of learning, when the person is particularly sensitive to criticism and must be encouraged and must encourage himself to chance certain endeavors. You can see this procedure operating in reverse when young art students are so jealous of their paintings, so serious about their performances, that they bridle when the teacher lays a brush upon their work.

In his fondest moments, the coach may believe that he has total control over the progress of his pupil. But the very character of coaching is likely to set into motion unpredictable changes of identity. The best model for visualizing this learning is not as a steady progression through a series of stages, mostly known to the coach, but rather to imagine a tree with many branches and twigs. The pupil moves along certain branches until he reaches alternatives, and the coach stands ready to guide or channel his movement until the next set of alternatives arises. But the best pupils, like the best children, get out from under the control and the vision of the best teachers, and the best teachers are pleased that this is so. At the outer limits of learning, the stages can no longer be as standardized as at the beginning; and the pupil discovers his own style, whether we are talking of religious conversion, musical composition, or anything else. For the coach, too, the process may be open-ended; he too may end with a different identity. This mutual change may be, as Nelson Foote has suggested, "a winning pattern for each,"[11] but unfortunately it may also be mutually destructive or end happily for one but not for the other.

Something should now be added to counteract the notion that coaching is merely a two-way relationship between a coach and a coached person, for many if not most coaching processes occur in organization or institutional context. Thus the teacher hands on pupils to higher or more famous teachers, saying "I can teach you no more, you are now beyond me—or at least it is said that you are beyond me." Although I shall not develop the point, you ought to recognize that the organizational framework within which the coaching goes on vitally affects the process and outcome of coaching. In some organizational contexts the coach may move his students too quickly (for his own fame, or to get them sponsored jobs), or his coaching may become standardized (because of great numbers of pupils, or because of the excessively strict requirements of the organization) or he may handle his pupils far too impersonally (because of personal tensions engendered by his position, or because of rewards placed upon other activities associated with his position). He may bind his students too closely to himself for their rapid or maximum development (because of his own anxieties created again by his position); or he may fail to sustain proper trust of himself (because close relationships among age ranks are frowned upon in the organization). Since coaching is thus linked with social structure and with the positions and careers of both the coaches and the coached, one can scarcely speak of process as divorced from structure. My discussion of process has been exceedingly general and its details must be spelled out in relation to particular structures and worlds. This is a task for meticulous and thoughtful research.

Dis-Identification and Identification: Brainwashing as a Case Study

Early in World War II the United States Government confronted its interned Japanese population with the necessity of signing an oath of allegiance to the country. Japanese-American citizens were faced with alternative choices of allegiance: to the United States or to Japan. They had to sign the oath or, after the war, be sent to Japan although most of them had never even visited there. Many refused to sign although they were loyal Americans, because the oath sometimes forced a razor sharp choice between signing or deserting their parents. Loyalty to nation—as Grodzins shows in his study of nationalism—may encompass, run parallel with, or run afoul of more specific group loyalties.[12]

The Japanese oath situation suggests the more usual covert contradictions that exist among loyalties. The government's branding of those who decided not to sign the oath as "disloyal" highlights the sacrifice and peril involved in any choice of sides. At crucial junctures you will find yourself lining up with some side against another—you must declare yourself. This is so whether the declaration is forced by an external agent, like the government, or by yourself during the silent battling of conscience. Consequent upon such declarations are the burning of bridges, the committing of irrevocable acts, and the forming of new allegiances. I have, in pages scattered throughout this essay, talked of sacrifice, loyalty, betrayal, danger, name-calling, motive and commitment; here I wish more explicitly to relate these to those radical shifts of identity that are in some measure coached, furthered, and forced by external agents.

As a striking and revealing illustration, consider the "brainwashing" of students by the Chinese government during the years following the Communist revolution. Brainwashing was, and is, essentially an attempt to destroy old loyalties, principally to family and social class, and to develop new loyalties to country and party. The tactics of this attempt at mass conversion doubtless varied with place and circumstance, but a number of standard procedures seem to have been used. These have been reported by the journalist, E. Hunter, in a suggestive and probably fairly reliable account.[13] Whether thoroughly accurate or not, this material will be useful for suggesting what is involved in forcing radical dis-identification; it is also useful for what it suggests about possible stages in moving from one set of loyalties to another.

During the first few months after arrival at a school, the students were engaged in day-long discussions of political and moral matters; in listening and taking careful notes of classroom lectures; in keeping diaries—open to inspection by their teachers—of their thoughts. To this was soon added "field work," consisting of labor in the fields so that they might experience the true value of labor. The class and group discussions turned, also, about further arranged experiences such as the witnessing of sometimes brutally executed punishment exacted from landlords by village peasants. "The girls who had broken into tears [over what

they had witnessed] were accused of warm-feelingism, of
'not knowing your friends from your enemies.' This kind
of sentimentality, the girls were told, should be cured by
self-criticism, for it was a dangerous defect in their characters."[14] Self-criticism was encouraged further by other
devices, among them the "thought seduction essay." This
consisted of a report about one's parents, grandparents, early
life, school experiences, friendships, and views on society.
Such reports were then discussed, dissected, and criticized
by others during the discussion sessions. The essay was com-
pared with earlier reports that one had written, and it was
pointed out to the student that his thought contained "deep
set contradictions." All the students were encouraged and
induced to talk publicly about themselves and their ideas.
Every student should talk if he has ideas, he should talk to
convince others who do not yet understand, he should do
this else it will be thought that he has no ideas. Those who
were reluctant to talk were thus pressured in a variety of
ways. Here is an instance of a linguistic device remarked
upon by one of Hunter's informants:

A subtle pressure is used against a person who does not enter the
discussion to the extent desired. In self-criticism sessions he called
a lagging-behind particle, a backward element, someone without
responsibility for the People's Revolution.[15]

Later the students were returned their essays and asked to
rewrite them according to what they now thought. This
latter composition was called a "thought conclusion essay."
It was read aloud in class and was subject to the usual comment and criticism. "Why had I gone out with a reactionary
girl? Have you slurred over your father's membership in a
Kuomintang organization? . . . Why have you not been
frank . . . and admitted that your mind was poisoned by
imperialist propaganda?"[16]

Many things can be said about this attempted process of
mass conversion. Hunter himself registers indignation at

the brutality and the perversion of thought involved in brainwashing. We would do better to conceive of it as a series of institutional strategies designed to unloosen people from old allegiances and to create proper new ones. Viewed from the side of the Communist Party, there are a number of devices that help accomplish this aim, and there are a number of agents who function at appropriate points to advise, counsel, pressure, castigate, coach, seduce, promise, and congratulate the candidate.

Several points are worth noting about the experiences of the candidate himself. During the initial phases of his conversion he is given a new vocabulary, by which he may rename and so re-evaluate objects and events. Political judgments become revised, but so do his judgments of his own actions. Discussion groups force him to declare his views, and institutional sanction is given to open attack upon them by his peers and superiors. The normally polite conventions of disagreement and innuendo are supplemented. Sanction is extended to public criticism of his past actions, and this criticism is made in the new political and social language. If the student is not altogether resistant, presumably he too is criticizing himself from these new standpoints. This involves him in a reassessment of his old motives; actions are now seen to have been committed for different reasons than were earlier believed. These motivational reassessments are couched in the new terminology. Such a device as making the candidate write an essay about his parents allows him to re-evaluate from new standpoints, what his parents actually are and were: misguided, corrupt, enemies of the people, or a member of a class that was alright in its day but is now opposing the people. When the authorities point out "deep contradictions" in his thought, they force a further self-review. If he has already begun to think in the new vocabulary, such contradictions will certainly exist. Discussions cause him also to recognize those contradictions which ordinarily he is not required to face. Normal processes of interaction whereby identities receive validation, or whereby a person may seek out and obtain such validation, are deliberately negated by the authorities and new bases for approval are substituted. We may hazard that turning points of great significance arise, including those that involve an overwhelming sense of betrayal to parents, friends, and to previous self. The importance of experiencing the institutionally arranged ordeals is clear. It is clear, too, that discussion groups serve as audiences for confessions and agents of confirmation when members pour out, in words, their ecstatic experiences.

What does not appear in Hunter's account of brainwashing, but which is suggested by descriptions of religious conversion, are such matters as backsliding and the resisting of temptation. Doubtless the authorities create temptations, for a man who has not overcome planned temptation can never be trusted not to succumb to accidental ones. Religious experience also suggests that the process of becoming dis-identified, hence disloyal, involves moments of intense anguish, a vague but meaningful term. Whatever else anguish may involve, it also involves the sense of being about to burn one's bridges: after the crucial act there is no turning back. Such moments of anguish are, of course, institutionally arranged, as when some students are asked to desert their parents and even their wives. It is at just such points of anguish and permanent decisive declaration that the candidate for conversion can also be lost, for when asked to line up irrevocably he finds he cannot do so.

Brainwashing, along with religious conversion, suggests that there are stages through which persons pass when undergoing a radical and fairly swift change of identity. Probably there is no universal sequence of steps: in fact, declaration, sacrifices, betrayals, and commitments of greater or lesser magnitude seem to be made all along the trajectory of the

conversion. Yet those institutional agencies deliberately seeking to promote conversion possess bodies of empirical rules
which include means that are to be used sequentially; certain things are desired, supposed, or expected to happen to
the candidate at certain times. Probably these sets of empirical rules change as institutional structures themselves
change.

Two errors are commonly made in thinking about conversion. One is that conversion is merely a question of
building loyalty toward something; whereas always it involves a loosening or abandoning of allegiances. People
sometimes appear to be ripe for conversion; this is only because their other loyalties are, or have grown, weak. Research
on the methods of the 19th-century American revivalists, by
R. R. Wohl,[17] shows that the revivalist did not breeze into
town and work miracles overnight, but used standard procedures for loosening up potential converts during two or
three days before the crucial day. A second misconception
about conversion is that when a person becomes partly converted, and then is "lost," he returns to his previous identity.
This is probably not so, for if a man has wandered some
way from his loyalties, it is doubtful whether he merely returns to them. As in brainwashing: once a man has absorbed
a new vocabulary with which to name and perceive the
world, including his own actions, he can scarcely tear the
vocabulary out of his brain; nor, even if he wishes to, can
he forget his most disloyal recent actions, such as the denun-
ciations of his family. Unlike relatively swift and radical
dis-identifications, slow seepage from bonds of allegiance
probably entails somewhat different processes; although betrayals, sacrifices, the resistance of temptations, and the like
should not be absent. But the thing that especially marks
the kind of personal crisis which I have just discussed, is the
alignment of such crises with their impersonal inducement
in institutional context.

Phases: Institutional and Personal

I wish now to turn, in closing this chapter on transformations of identity, to temporary, if patterned, changes of persons and their behavior. "Temporary" is terminologically related to "temporal" and "time." The vocabularies of all societies cut and order the flow of time, and as Everett Hughes has called to our attention,[18] when a society divides time into conventional units it thereby succeeds in introducing periodicities, repetitions, routines and high points into the lives of its members. During and associated with these periods—whether moments, hours, episodes, or seasons—certain acts are supposed to be performed, others are tabooed, and others are allowed providing anyone should avail himself of the opportunity. Quite clearly this affects the course of interactions.

Turn this statement of institutional action into a statement of identity, and you would say that people are sanctioned to *be* different during different periods. The way to act during a celebration is as a celebrant; the way to act during a legal cross-examination is as accused, accuser, or witness. A status, as I remarked earlier, is likely to become a way of being as well as a way of acting.

A temporal dimension is implicit in all kinds of status. No one is assigned, nor may he assume, a position or status for ever. Always there is a clause, whether hidden or openly acknowledged, whereby a man may be dispossessed or may dispossess himself of the status. Some statuses, as Nelson Foote has appropriately remarked, are socially "scheduled"; people enter and leave them at scheduled times, and generally from other positions while moving toward still others. "Social scheduling is like a game of musical chairs, except that people know in advance when the next change is coming, and as a rule no one gets left out."[19] In less regulated mobility, people take up and drop positions in no particular order; but whether the status is assumed progressively, sporadically, or periodically, these very adverbs suggest the notion of a time period. A great many of these are named in the vocabularies of social chronology. During them people are licensed, obligated, sanctioned and tabooed beings.

The matter of a temporal identity is made much more complicated because kinds of status themselves possess a scheduled inner structure. By this I mean merely that people are always entering and leaving them; also that people are always at one point or another in their occupancy. A convenient illustration is the Presidency of the United States, for it is clearly recognized that a President during his fourth year is in a different phase than during his first or sixth. Harold Laski has gone so far as to suggest that a President in his fourth year who is seeking re-election is, in fact, mainly engaged in seeking re-election.[20] If such "phases" are sufficiently recurrent, they are likely to receive names. Although the steps of entrance, passage through, and exit from a status are not always perfectly clear, this phase-like character of status is worth analyzing. For this purpose, an established time period like mourning—with its sharp beginning but somewhat blurred ending—will be useful.

Typically, mourning is designed to do something both for the mourner and the mourned. The former is licensed to ignore or forbidden to meet certain daily obligations, such as going to his office or attending social affairs. Thus the dead receive deference and the bereaved are, in effect, drawn out of ordinary social circulation. Certain actions of the mourner can be discounted because he is "not himself," particularly during the early phases of his bereavement. For the same reason there are also institutionally permitted moments when the mourner may claim great privacy. If his grief appears too overwhelming, agents support him through this period of tribulation; they know what to do, more or less, because

certain remedies have been found effective. When the bereaved enters again into more ordinary kinds of interaction
—as he passes to later, less deep phases of mourning—he
bears marks upon his clothing, or otherwise signalizes his
condition so that others are warned. When such signs are not
made or are overlooked, awkward and embarrassing moments occur. Implicit during the entire period are stages,
running from the initial shock of grief to the termination
of mourning when all incident is supposed to be under control and the mourner is more or less himself again. If he
stays too long in a deep state of grief, then he violates social
expectations and his relatives are prone to call upon the
doctor or other counselors. Conversely, if he does not remain
long enough in the status of mourner or moves too fast
through its phases, he invites criticism.

For our purposes several points about this traditional
status are especially noteworthy. Although practices vary tremendously the world over, it is characteristic that the period
of mourning consists of these transitions or phases. They
are signalized in traditional ways, either by the mourner or
by others or by both. Spatial features enter: thus, deep grief
is expressed appropriately in certain sites—before the bier,
at the open grave, in the privacy of one's bedroom. The re-
moval of the bereaved from some requirements of ordinary
discourse is notable but often, so is the speed of his return
to daily life. Extraordinary circumstances can speed up the
phases of mourning or cut them short, and indeed when
mourning customs are in flux the requirements of business
life tend to do precisely this. All in all, since the person
acts or is supposed to act differently in one phase than in
another, it is essential that others know what phase he is in
and that he signal this information to them. He must, in
effect, identify himself for them.

We could similarly describe any number of other con-

ventional periods: honeymoons, fasting days, feast days, celebrations, vacations, purification rites, jury deliberations, pa-
role. Some of these conventional time spans are periodic,
others happen only once. What marks them all is that there
are well established signs of when a person is supposed to go
into the phase, how he and you are to recognize that he is
in it, how long he is expected to remain there, by what
signs you can recognize that he is beginning to emerge from
the phase, and when he is thoroughly "over" it.

All groups recognize periods of time which, though they
are much less institutionalized than those mentioned above,
are yet conventionalized. In families, for instance, the parents may render the child incommunicado as a punishment:
he must remove himself physically from interaction, must
refrain from doing certain things and must by command
do another, such as meditate upon his transgression; and his
re-entry into communication is preceded at least by some
stated period of isolation or by a rite of apology. Punishment
by isolation is generally less of a routine in family life than
the one o'clock rest period, but it is, nevertheless, rather
well governed by conventional understandings.

Such understandings are multitudinous, and can be drawn
upon at will, as when one enters voluntarily upon some
transitory phase. You signal that you have a headache, and
will withdraw, or will listen but not actively participate in
conversation. You may even go to sleep in public with the
understanding, in some groups at least, that you are not to
be disturbed. (I have heard jazz musicians use the suggestive
phrase "to fall out.") Asked a question, you may declare
yourself "in thought," not to be disturbed or asked further
questions until you signal your return to the conversation.
Such incidents suggest that all that you must do to elicit
appropriate action from others is to announce your entrance
into certain phases; you are given exemption, license, but

also appropriate obligations: having slept, the sleeper is supposed to be refreshed; having thought, the thinker is supposed to have answers.

Viewed more longitudinally, interaction is punctuated by much longer phases than mere withdrawal from conversation for thought and sleep. A student may withdraw from a busy social life for several weeks to study for exams or to go on a prolonged reading kick. Conversely, he may plunge periodically into a social whirl. Erik Erikson has pointed to an eight year period in the life of G. B. Shaw during which the great man declared a virtual moratorium on all ordinary commitments.[21] He resigned from a business post, at which he was by ordinary standards successful, left family and friends, left Ireland for England, and, as Shaw says, "left a phase behind me, and associated no more with men my age until, after about eight years of solitude in this respect, I was drawn into the Socialist revival of the early eighties." He meanwhile employed himself in learning to write, which meant in the deeper sense, as both Shaw's account and Erikson's commentary make clear, utilizing his moratorium to work out a new sense of identity. Shaw is not alone; many people declare moratoria, albeit less radical ones. They also declare periods for the consolidation of psychological gains, periods for resting upon laurels after success, periods for personal trial or probation, periods for expatiation of sins, periods for contemplation, periods for prolonged self-searching. All such periods, which themselves also consist of a series of phases, are much less institutionalized than are honeymoons, celebrations, and other such regulated episodes. Nevertheless, a person may often utilize conventional signs to indicate that he is entering, or is in the midst of such a period, and wishes to have his claims to it honored.

There is always the potential problem of legitimizing one's right to enter a phase that is not clearly institutionalized, for the signs adduced then for placement of self can be debated. School children thus sometimes encounter difficulties when trying to receive authorization to leave school grounds before dismissal time, unless they can produce unequivocal signs of illness; and some are compelled to remain when seriously, although not violently, sick. Legitimation is rendered easier when the claim to a phase conforms traditionally to what is expected at a given age. A young man is freer to wander aimlessly or to experiment with jobs than a middle-aged one. Legitimation is linked in this way with timing, as phases run athwart other phases. When phases are part of lengthier temporal periods, there is always the possibility that people may too quickly or too slowly pass through these periods. Any extraordinary pace must be justified. The patient who argues that he is sicker than the doctor thinks, and the patient who insists on getting out of bed before it seems that he should, are both bothersome to the doctor.

Actually, although I have been writing as if people were passing through a single phase at any given time, this is never so. Even in grief and deep mourning you only temporarily lay aside your other temporal identities, and during an extended period of mourning, you continually interrupt it to enter into quite different phases. Life consists not merely in adjudicating between the demands of stable kinds of status, but also in juggling differential temporal placement. On Monday morning, you may be entering the initial phase of one status, leaving another, and be midstream in several others. To which should you pay chief attention? The query suggests problems of self-legitimation and self-justification. These can never be fully or finally resolved, for you are forever moving on into new phases.

Among the most important are those that are associated with major changes of identity. These are crucial phases in any man's life. Shaw's extended moratorium, as Erikson makes clear, allowed him to move from one type of world, one type of identity, to a new world and identity without causing an absolute break between his past and his present. Erikson, in fact, suggests that in American society the adolescent transition to adulthood has something of the quality of a similar moratorium, or period of experimental and relatively unobligated license before adolescents settle into adult status.[22] People sometimes remove themselves physically for extended periods to "retreats," to think out problems of identity, emerging with revelations, societal or personal. We all do this on a smaller scale when we seize moments of privacy and contemplation. On the other hand, there are crucial phases in our lives that involve furious social mingling and extensive communicative contacts, as when we require immediate and strong support of failing self-images or when we need to validate and re-validate new found conceptions of ourselves. It is possible that periods of rapid learning are closely linked with such phases. This is explicitly pointed out by Sullivan, who remarks upon the considerable change that may occur immediately after children have passed over the "threshholds of a developmental era."[23] It is important to recognize that although you may intuitively sense the phase you are most "in," you do not necessarily know or name it accurately. Presumably you must learn to know what your phases "mean," what they "are." A phase can be misnamed because you are not skilled at knowing it or because someone else's definition appears more trustworthy.

Since a person is, during a crucial phase, quite literally a different person than when he was not, it is necessary that others, if they are to handle him skillfully, must learn to recognize such phases. They must read the signs correctly, whether such signs are indexes—that is, symptoms—or whether the person himself signals his state. Recognition of phase is furthered by subsidiary cues, such as information about the man's career and life cycle, so that the current "him" can be placed against the background of his probable other phases. Skills in this interactional game vary tremendously, so that some people are quite blind to others' phases and suffer the consequences, while some cash in on their own astute guesses. (Of course, too great an insight into another's phase may sometimes prevent one from making the demands and claims of less sensitive observers.) People also vary in the skills they possess for signaling their phases.

Consider also, as a final consideration, that the observer himself is human and therefore is going through phases also. Interaction is between people who are "in phases"—differential ones. In sociological research we crudely recognize this by talking of contact between people in different stages of learning, or of people who are experiencing different occupational tensions, with consequences to their handling of each other. A more explicit recognition of phases *in* interaction —not merely phases *of* interaction—would be useful.

CHAPTER FIVE

Change and Continuity

Generational Relations and Personality Development

I HAVE led you through many pages in attempting to deal with changes of identity through adulthood, as seen from a sociological frame of reference. Implicit in this framework, also, is a critique of extant theories of personality development insofar as they oversimplify relationships between the person and his significant others. I am far less interested in a critique than in suggesting certain leads for studying new dimensions of self-other relations.

I wish to suggest now, in this chapter, certain ways of viewing the relations between self and significant others, ways implicit in the sociological orientation, and also to speculate on matters of "actual" or "experienced" personal continuity.

But first, a few words of comment on theories of personality development might be useful as an initial orientation. All these theories are, explicitly or implicitly, but more often explicitly, theories about the most significant relations assumed to exist among members of the same and different generations. Perhaps this is not more often recognized because most developmental accounts are couched in terms of the interpersonal relations of children and their parents, children and their sibs, children and certain peers, and children and family surrogates. In psychoanalytic theory, the maturation of the child's body through a series of stages,

and the very title of "psychosexual theory," further tend to
obscure some implicit premises about generational relations;
but in the writing of H. S. Sullivan—with his stress upon
the sequential importance of parents, playmates, chums,
girl friends, and lovers—the generational aspect is more
apparent, if not stressed. In anthropological writings on
"culture and personality" much is said, of course, about how
the different peers and adult agents (whether family members or not) help socialize the child. But in almost all
accounts of development, personality is more or less taken
as completed by late adolescence. Hence a more systematic
scrutiny is probably not made of relations existing between
or among all generations that are alive during a person's
lifetime. Yet you must ask, if you take seriously much of
what I have written, what relevance these relations have for
the formation and change of identities—at any age.

A well regulated set of status-passages, graded upward
by age, of the sort previously touched upon, yields a rather
static, non-historical picture of a life cycle. The passage of
each generation through those steps of status is similar, in all
significant regards, to that of the preceding generations. To
obtain the typical picture we merely must ask—as in Arensberg's Irish countryman description[1]—what personages are
most important, during each age span, to the Irishman: his
mother, father, grandparents, brothers, age mates, wife, or
children. Their relative influences may vary throughout his
lifetime in socially patterned ways. Likewise, such a detailed
account of age-grading as is found in W. Lloyd Warner's
Black Civilization[2] demonstrates how a man's teachers—in
the large sense—may vary in status, and the varied content of
what they teach, throughout his life cycle. Such monographs
are not designed to show that the experience of one generation is much different than that of the generations preceding
and succeeding it; but to specify with precision how relations among generations are patterned. An age-grading de-

scription does not ordinarily—though it conceivably can—
raise the question of what impact one generation makes upon
a second and consequently what differential impact the second makes upon a third; and, I should be able to add without
being thought facetious, how the third might then influence
the life of the first. Presumably in a world where "A youngster sees his probable future career in the activities that
others of his sex perform . . . sequences that he too will go
through when he is older,"[3] not much account need be taken
of generational differences, but only of generational relations as they form each generation in the image of its
predecessor.

   In the United States—where, as a study by Stendler shows,
we have had several wide swings of child rearing practice
during the past sixty years—we need to take generational
differences into account.[4] Indeed, for over a century there
has been a suggestive body of philosophical and sociological
speculation about generations: their identities, oppositions
and orientations.[5] Heidegger, the German existentialist philosopher, was struck with the fatefulness of the links between
persons of approximately the same age: "The inescapable
fate of living in and with one's generation completes the
full drama of individual human existence."[6] Pinder, an art
historian, spelled out even more explicitly the possible rele-
vancy of generational position for identity:

Everyone lives with people of the same and of different ages, with
a variety of possibilities of experience facing them all alike. But
for each the same 'time' is a different time—that is, it represents
a different period of his self, which he can only share with people
of his own age.[7]

You need not agree with everything in these quotes to recognize that the model of a regulated, and rather unchanging,
series of age-graded passages of status is far too simple a
model to be very useful for studying modern societies. It
is too simple even for studying a primitive people who have

been invaded by outsiders. A wonderfully suggestive treatment of generational differences by an observer of French colonial life, O. Mannoni, will afford us material for building the more complex model that is needed.

Mannoni, writing of "the succession of generations" in Madagascar, points out that the French settled the island over fifty years ago, quite succeeding in imposing white domination over the natives.[8] The latter were, on the whole, satisfied with the state of affairs. One reason for their placid acceptance was that the social structure of the island was not conceived as having changed drastically. The native organization of authority was transferred fairly easily from tribe and family to the French, so that no great disorganization of tribal life occurred. The natives were eager, also, to learn the ways and skills of the French. However their children—who were not yet adults when the first settlers appeared—have been reared in a far different milieu. Their parents, as I have noted, had transferred authority to the French so that the French were always part of their world; and western education was available in some form to many. Some of the younger people have become "uprooted"; they have broken away in some degree from tribal ways, yet paradoxically yearn for the old days and the old freedoms. Despite revivalistic aspirations, these younger natives are a tremendous force making for further change in tribal organization. They are regarded with "a certain fascination" even by many of the tradition-oriented elders. Until the preceding decade (Mannoni wrote in 1950) the models of the native youth were derived from the tradition-oriented generation, but these models are no longer influential.

Mannoni's picture of the French side of Madagascar society is equally complex. The original settlers were self-assured people, dominant over the natives and patriarchical toward their children. The children, now adults, bear the marks of their current difficult situation. On the one hand they feel inferior toward their parents; and on the other, they are supposed to be absolutely superior to the natives. But their relations with the latter are complex because they feel basically insecure as men. Furthermore, they share their dominant social position on Madagascar with other Frencchmen who, like the original settlers, were born in France. Toward these "metropolitans," the island-born Frenchman feels superior but he also feels antagonistic. The psychological relations of the metropolitan French toward the native Madagascans are understandably less complex than those of the colonial French.

In this description, more generational relations are left implicit than are explicitly stated—the accuracy of Mannoni's description quite aside. Let us review first what is explicit. Some generational relations are described *vertically*: those existing between French settlers and their children; between the original natives and their children; and, in passing, relations between the native children and their grandparents. All these relations are viewed as running both ways: younger to older, also older to younger. The generational relations on the island are also described *horizontally*: between French settlers (first generation) and the natives (first generation); between metropolitans and island-born French; between both types of colonials and the current native adults. Nevertheless, if we are interested in who, on the island, are significant others to whom, in what ways, and how so, then horizontal and vertical dimensions, as Mannoni sketchily gives them, need to be much supplemented. We need information also about *diagonal* relations, for instance those between second generation natives and first generation French. We do not know whether the metropolitans appear significantly different to the uprooted natives than the second generation, island-born, French; nor whether the natives, now, are reacting toward the French in terms of their previous youthful contacts with first generation Frenchmen. The analysis given us by Mannoni of precisely where the generational lines fall is also blurred. And it is probable that he has overlooked various important segments of native and French society. We should, in a fuller analysis, wish also to know whether other important variables may condition actual and fantasy contact between these social segments; for instance, is there much social differentiation among natives, or among colonials, and does this affect contact across the "same" generation? Uprooted native men may possess rather different significant others than uprooted native women—each other for instance—or the latter may have followed chronologically the appearance of uprooted men, and have been tutored by them. What we are asking is a series of detailed queries turning about whom is significant in whose world: this no one knows beforehand, although some fairly systematic guesses can be made.

Even so, we should not commit the error of believing that we are talking about Madagascar society during more than a single era of its history. The very emergence of a third and fourth generation will vastly multiply the potentially different kinds of significant others (for instance, if natives marry with, or employ, colonials) for all living generations; and who of what age is important to whom at a given age will be far from easily predictable.

The Madagascar situation is, in a far simpler way, reminiscent of the historical emergence of Hawaiian society. There, the whites long ago invaded, dominated, and married native Hawaiians. After some years, the whites imported successive waves of immigrant plantation workers: at first the Chinese, then the Japanese, then others (Korean, Puerto Rican, Filipino). The first generation of Chinese produced Chinese and Chinese-Hawaiian children. The Japanese immigrants produced Japanese, Japanese-Chinese, and Japanese-Hawaiian children. Meanwhile the Chinese-Hawaiians were marrying Hawaiians and Chinese-Hawaiians, but were experienc-

ing some difficulty in attempting to marry Chinese for the
Chinese population had begun to erect social barriers against
outsiders. This complicated and chronologically unstable
generational picture—although striking because of its racial
and intermarital aspects—is probably not so very much more
complex, indeed possibly less so, than can be found in many
another milieu.

The complicated model of generational relations that then
emerges suggests more than merely that theories of personality development operate with oversimplified models. "Age"
is clearly a major variable in considering such change and
development; but across the span of your life different significant others may come and go, may wax and wane in importance. My amplified, sociological, model suggests that this
waxing and waning is not altogether indeterminate, accidental, but is socially and complexly patterned. The age of the
important others as related to your own age is not merely
a matter of age; but of race, nationality, social class, social
status, sex, and a host of other variables. But the world is
different for persons of different age and generation even
if they share in common, sex, class, and nationality, and
occupation.

Some of the earlier writers wrestled with such problems
as whether persons of one generation, regardless of class or
sex, had more in common with each other than with other
generations; and whether it made a difference that a generation was conscious of its commonness of position and experience. The sociologist today would tend to say that in some
countries people of, say, the same social class but of different
generations have much more "in common" than persons of
the same generation but of different social class; on the other
hand, many young women in underdeveloped countries who
are in revolt against their traditional female status appear
to have very much in common. Our discussion has led us
to add that not only must we look and see, in particular

places and times, but that these matters may change within the lifetimes of those whom we are studying. There is one joker in the sociological deck that ought to be recognized as such: differences and similarities of age are not objectively fixed—unless you merely define generations as every person born within the same decade. Definitions of who is approximately of the same age, who is much older or a little older, who is almost as old or somewhat younger, are all social categories, hence changeable. With whom you are identified in age is neither a static definition, nor unrelated to the social structures in which you have membership.

What then are some of the more general implications of this position that I have taken on generational contact and influence—other than that theories of personality development are too simple? Anthropologists who were interested in personality formerly criticized Freudian theory on grounds of its inadequate coverage of cultural differences, and now one might wryly protest that anthropologists are being criticized because of inadequate coverage of historical differences. Yet the "quest for certainty" about universal processes of personality development is likely to continue—and in a sense there is no reason why it should not continue providing we recognize how far we are from achieving certainty. There are several clear implications flowing from the sociological model sketched above. One, of course, is that we consider seriously the possibility that general development continues long after adolescence. Another, is that personality theories ought not to hide behind the notion that changes in later life are merely variants of earlier, more basic, developments. The pertinent question is not how basic the changes might be in the abstract, but to whom they occur, under what conditions, and of what kinds they are.

A less obvious implication is that one premise underlying psychiatric accounts of development might well be abandoned—or at least held hypothetically in abeyance. This premise is that there are certain steps through which the human organism must pass to become more or less mentally healthy, adapted to reality, and adjusted to social life. This seems, of course, a very reasonable premise; but its assumption ties developmental accounts to bodily maturation, to inevitable and hidden premises about the nature of healthy functioning, and very probably to culture-bound norms as to this functioning. At the very least the assumption directs attention away from "the normal."

What I am saying is not that the psychiatric model of development is not useful, but that a different kind of model, worked out in detail, should complement the psychiatric one. The latter can be represented—to use a visual metaphor —as something like a fir tree: the trunk is the main line of normal development, and the branches signify all possible variations of maladjustment. The psychiatrist focuses sharply upon when and how these maladjustments occur, as well as upon the proper interpersonal conditions which allow a person to move from stage to stage (up the trunk). Unless these interpersonal conditions are met, the individual's development becomes arrested; he does not go up along the entire main trunk but out along one of the lower branches.

The sociological model is more reminiscent of a constantly unrolling Japanese scroll. Upon it are painted the society's age-grades, carefully subdivided by dozens of relevant sociological variables. The scroll, unlike the more static anthropological type of picture, is on one side constantly unrolling (the future) and rolling up (the past) on the other. Generation succeeds generation, new ones appear and old ones disappear, and living generations change in process. From the sociological perspective, as in the psychiatric, problems of identity are to the forefront—including tortured identities —but the approach to these problems is necessarily different; much as the sociological perspective upon interaction owes something to the psychiatric, but necessarily differs from it.

The Minimizing of Identity Change

In an essay on identity there ought to be comment, however brief, about how identity may remain relatively unchanged over considerable spans of time. Traditionally, this question is handled under the rubric of "the stability of personality"; and the answers run a gamut from genuine biological explanations (body types, glandular functioning) through quasi-biological ones (drives, needs), to certain unifying forces "within" the person that serve to explain persistent behavior (traits, the need for self-realization).

Sociologists generally assume, or maintain, that the more stable the social environment, the more probable will be the stability of behavior and person. But the composite term "stable environment" is far from unambiguous. "Environment" refers not merely to an objective world, "out there," but also to the world as experienced. Oversights occur when the subjective side of this relationship is disregarded. For instance, for many years sociologists have regarded urban life as disorganizing; thereby underemphasizing, and often quite neglecting the fact that many urbanites have lived in fairly "expected" environments. Even in a milieu marked by rapid social change, men seize opportunities for forestalling and minimizing personal change; they appear to establish, with at least partial success, islands of stability.

The psychiatrists and clinical psychologists have paid special attention to the more pathological, and unconscious, forms of controlling interaction that result in minimizing personality change. It is useful to have descriptions of the personal mechanisms whereby men avoid entering certain face-to-face interactions and seek to transform others into kinds which they can better control. An advancement is made upon the complex question of how identities are maintained when the psychiatric orientation is supplemented by analysis of the more institutional, cultural, as well as the more deliberately calculated personal means of minimizing change.

In general, it is true that great and prolonged disjunctures in ordinary social life—internment in concentration camps or downward mobility during revolutions and economic depressions—maximize the possibility of the unexpected and the shattering. At the opposite pole, a quiet progression of institutionalized statuses from cradle to grave hardly insures an unchanging identity; but it does prevent those radical crises during which options multiply and group rationales become inadequate for handling personal dilemmas. Likewise, various conventional explanations for sloughing off aspects of past behavior—such as "interests" which notoriously change during a lifetime—prevent a person questioning the change, and thereby prevent further questioning of himself. This sloughing off of the past is more like paring nails than losing a limb.

Add now the possibility that social tasks become fitted more or less to recognized abilities; that is, a man with proven training and abilities tends to be used in similar capacities repeatedly. This is one of the consequences of acquiring a reputation. But a reputation also prevents him from being engaged for those tasks wherein he is a proven, or suspected, failure. Of course, this implies that there exists a large reservoir of unrecognized ability in persons who are thus repeatedly assigned tasks and positions. Aside from deliberate and shrewd disguise, there are reasons why potential is overlooked; among them are these: that a man is not brought into contact with those who could help him develop it; that even if signs of certain abilities exist, the

signs are not visible to, or are incorrectly read, by his associates; and there may be, quite literally, no means available
for detecting a certain kind of ability because its expression
lies in the future.

We may speculate further that the social fabric allows
fair latitude for those personal choices that reduce the possibility of disjunctive and challenging experiences. From the
whole array of groups and organizations which surround and
confront you, you may seek, wittingly or not, to choose com-
patible memberships, or voluntarily withdraw from those
groups that disturb you. Within divergent organizations the
jobs that you seek to do, the positions that you seek to fill,
can be manipulated so that their demands are rendered more
or less consonant. Many occupational careers conspicuously
exhibit such patterning. There is too, as I have already remarked, a time dimension involved in memberships: so that
if hurt, threatened, insulted, disappointed, you may withdraw from one position; but you can also withdraw temporarily and throw energies into other endeavors. After the
phase has run to completion, you may turn back to what you
found offensive or threatening. Thus the occupancy of positions is not only multiple but sequential and timed. We
might think of this as a kind of immunization through positional maneuvering. Do not make the mistake of supposing
that such maneuvering is necessarily unconscious; it may
be utilized as a deliberate and flexible tactic by people who
recognize their own phases with accompanying weaknesses
and strengths.

Memberships can also be built or earned, rather than
applied for or assigned. Rejected from an organization or
rejecting it, a strong or obstinate man can create his own
organization according to his own images and tastes. Around
him he can gather those supporters who validate his conception of himself; thus he protects himself from corrosive
criticism, as well as from perversely frightening promises

of liberation from a current self. All in all, the more swiftly changing the society, the more requisite it is for a person— in one way or another—to rely upon his skills at selecting and balancing group memberships in order to maintain the fact and sense of personal continuity.

The usual sociological analysis of personal dilemmas stresses this balancing and selecting under such subject matters as the "incompatibility of roles" and the "failure to meet role expectations." The few remarks I have hazarded about the institutional conditions furthering personal stability suggest that a more historically-minded approach is needed. By this I mean not merely that people undergo more radical changes under drastic social conditions or during certain periods of life, but that social structures themselves have histories and the fate of their members is correspondingly affected. If, for instance, a field of medical specialization is marked by rapid expansion, it offers its recruits exciting and dangerous experiences; but a specialty bearing an identical name twenty years later, grown "mature" and relatively static, may provide its practitioners with a rather quiet milieu. The role incompatibilities and dilemmas within such a specialty arise out of, and affect, its history and the histories of associated specialties. In the next chapter of this essay, I shall elaborate upon both the symbolic character of group membership and its historical aspects. Before doing this, I wish to consider something allied with, but different from, the persistence of behavior—the sense or recognition of changes in one's identity.

The Sense of Personal Continuity

The persistence of identity is quite another thing than its imagined persistence. In Erikson's terminology there is a difference between "a conscious sense of individual identity" and "an unconscious striving for a continuity of personal character," or between the former and "the silent doings of ego-synthesis."[9]

Some of the conditions for the actual minimization of change, of course, have relevance for a person's lack of recognition of change in himself. A prefigured life-cycle, a standardized progression of social positions, not only actually minimizes crises but obscures those changes that occur and aids in explaining them away. The very names for a given status, as well as the presumed coherent complex of associated tasks, helps to dull any sense of personal change even when the actual behavior associated with the status becomes altered.

Through the years, much that a person recognizes as belonging characteristically to himself—as for instance an intense liking for foods characteristic of his ethnic group—obscures recognition of other, seemingly less important, shifts in taste and conduct. Awareness of significant change is a symbolic matter. A change must be deemed important before it and kindred changes can be perceived as vitally important. Everyone's behavior changes in some regard but not in all; and which changes are worth taking into special account and which are trifling, peripheral, irrelevant, and even believed spurious does not depend merely upon the appearance or disappearance of actual behavior.

Each person's account of his life, as he writes or thinks about it, is a symbolic ordering of events. The sense that you make of your own life rests upon what concepts, what interpretations, you bring to bear upon the multitudinous and disorderly crowd of past acts. If your interpretations are convincing to yourself, if you trust your terminology, then there is some kind of continuous meaning assigned to your life as-a-whole. Different motives may be seen to have driven you at different periods, but the overriding purpose of your life may yet seem to retain a certain unity and coherence.

Thus, a late convert to a sect may view most of his life as actually spent in the service of the Lord and regard the early wastrel years as a necessary preparation to the later service; or certain events may stand out as deviant from the general stream of a career, thereby contributing, by their very rarity, a further unity to the main line. The deviant events may be discounted because they belong to earlier or more youthful phases.

He thought of it as a youthful folly. He put his vote for Eugene Debs alongside his visit to a parlor house when he was twenty. Both were things he expected of growing boys.[10]

Deviant events may be explained also as temptations, as illnesses, escapes, releases, last minute flings, and foolhardiness. Like other assignments of motive and meaning, those made about one's own self may—indeed must—change over the years. With new experiences, everyone discovers new meanings and orderings in his career.

Such terminological assessment is crucial to feelings of continuity or discontinuity. If past acts appear to fit together more or less within some scheme, adding up to and leading up to the current self, then "they were me, belong to me, even though I have somewhat changed." It is as if you were to tell the story of your life, epoch by epoch, making sense of each in terms of the end product. The subjective feeling of continuity turns not merely upon the number or degree of behavioral changes, but upon the framework of terms within which otherwise discordant events can be reconciled and related. Past purposes and dedications may be challenged and abandoned, but when viewed as part of a larger temporal design they do not plague one by feelings of self-betrayal. It is the very lack of design that is reflected subjectively in feelings of personal discontinuity, of wrecked or abandoned selves, or more mildly experienced in the lack of meaningful purposes, in conceptions of certain periods of one's life that were wasted, or senseless, or did not lead anywhere. Past identities can be reconciled, made to appear uniform despite their apparent diversity, only if they can be encompassed in a unified interpretation. A firm sense of one-ness rests upon "coming to terms with self"—a suggestive pun. The terms of settlement are never over and done with; the point is magnificently illustrated by the ending of Balzac's *Père Goriot,* when an elderly man upon his deathbed almost questions his entire life, as he stands upon the brink of rec-ognizing an abrupt transformation of self, but is released from confronting himself full-face by death.[11]

The awareness of constancy in identity is, then, in the eye of the beholder rather than "in" the behavior itself. The point holds no less for biography than for autobiog-raphy. Camus has said:

Looking at these existences from the outside, one lends them a coherence and unity which, in truth, they cannot have, but which appears evident to the observer. He sees only the outline of these lives, without taking account of the complicating detail.[12]

But the point is not merely that the observer misses com-plicating detail; it is that events must be ordered to be comprehended at all. Like other events, the details of any person's life may be conceptually organized and patterned by the observer and thus understood, explained, and man-aged. "We make art out of these [observed] existences."[13] Different biographers organize more or less the same facts bearing upon someone's actions, and each arrives at a fairly unified but not necessarily congruent picture of the hero and the course of his life. Neither the biographer, nor the auto-biographer can afford to admit that more than a few of these puzzling, poorly understood, actions are vitally im-portant to the personal narrative. If they seem important, they will be woven somehow into the story—else disjuncture will be recognized and gaps sensed.

CHAPTER SIX

Membership and History

IN THIS last chapter, I wish to call attention to certain characteristics of group membership that stem from its symbolic character. My focus is upon the relation of person to group, rather than upon an examination of group structure, although some of my remarks surely have implications for the latter interest. Here I shall bring you full circle to the opening theme of the essay—the central role of language for identity—although each section ought to be recognizably connected with that theme. In this chapter I shall stress also the necessity for historical research in studies of membership and identity.

Membership as a Symbolic Matter[1]

Group life is organized around communication. Communication consists not merely in the transmission of ideas from the head of one person to that of another, it signifies shared meanings. "Shared" means more than that terms are used in ways sufficiently alike so that persons understand each other; it also means that terms arise out of and in turn permit community action. As Dewey has written, language

compels one individual to take the standpoint of other individuals and to see and inquire from a standpoint that is . . . common to them as participants or "parties" in a conjoint undertaking.

. . . The physical sound gets its meaning in and by conjoint community of functional use.[2]

We might speak of a group that consisted of only two members provided they were to act conjointly, with consensus, because they shared important symbols. Popular idiom does not usually refer to groups of two persons, but the principle involved is the same whether the groups have three members, ten, one hundred, or more. The members are able to participate in various coordinated activities because they share a common terminology. Groups form around points of agreement, and then new classifications arise on the basis of further shared experience.

The constitution of any human group is thus a symbolic, not a physical fact. This is obvious, of course, when one considers such groups as the United Nations or the Democratic Party; but it is equally true of the Smith family, the American Negro, or the United States. A family is composed of more than blood members and is hardly dependent upon the face-to-face contact of all its members. A man is a Negro not merely or even necessarily because of skin color. As for a nation, 150,000,000 persons scarcely constitute a unit merely because of geographic proximity. Geographical and biological considerations may contribute to the formation of concepts and may in some sense enter into the concepts themselves—for the members of a nation conceive of themselves as occupying a common territory and sometimes as stemming from a common ancestry. But groups exist as such only because of the common symbolizations of their members. Many or most groups are easily visualized in purely symbolic terms since they are less directly connected with geography and biology than are nation and family.

The symbolic nature of groups raises intricate questions concerning membership. If one takes membership to mean only formal "joining," no great question arises concerning membership in certain kinds of groups. You either are, or

are not, a Rotarian or a Senator. But clearly the formal criteria are not sufficient. In a more subtle sense, you may
belong but not have much allegiance, not participate much,
and you may not actually belong but participate a good deal.
To ticket a man as formally holding membership in such
and such groups barely suggests the nature and quality of
his allegiances.

When a group is small, it is usually possible to determine
the outer limits of its membership, although even then difficulties may be encountered. But when a group is large, and
especially when it is not territorially fixed, then genuine
practical and theoretical questions arise concerning who
really does belong and upon whom the group may rely for
what. Is a man a Lutheran if he has not been to church for
twenty years? Is a man always a Catholic in some sense, even
though he may have been excommunicated (a significant
word) or have left the Church? If a gentile woman marries a
Jew and embraces his faith, is she or is she not a Jewess? Suppose that she divorces him but continues to attend synagogue
services regularly and raises her children as Jews, is she still
Jewish? If he in turn grows unreligious and associates with
fewer Jewish people than she does, who is the more Jewish
or the more truly Jewish of the two? Likewise, if a Negro
passes for a number of years as white, is he still a Negro,
particularly if he now names or identifies himself as white?
If a "white" mixes with Negroes to the extent that he thinks
about most racial issues as they do, to what extent is he still,
conventionally speaking, white? These are not extreme cases,
for membership and allegiance often are just that elusive.

Sometimes social scientists draw distinctions between
"membership" and "reference" groups, attempting to take
into account two situations: membership without much
participation, and participation without membership. Thus
Sherif has defined a membership group as one in which an

individual "is an actual member" and a reference group as one from which

the individual's standards, attitudes and status aspiration stem. . . . In many cases his reference groups are groups of which he is an actual member. . . . But this is not always so. He may be actually a member of one group, but through his contact with the attitudes and aspirations of another he may do his best to relate himself, his standards, his aspirations to that group.[3]

The phrase "groups of which he is an actual member" can signify only formal membership, or membership in a group so well structured that its members know of each other. Membership group and reference group are, in fact, such an over-simplification of the facts of social life that it is possible to find one writer (Sherif) sharply criticizing others (Merton and Kitt) for writing that enlisted men in the Army were "positively oriented to the norms of a group of which they were not members, that is the norms of the officers." Sherif has maintained that "the army organization and its officers serve as a reference group for such enlisted men and not the informal groups that emerged among their fellow enlisted men."[4] Merton and Kitt, though committed to the distinction, themselves write that

There is nothing fixed about the boundaries separating . . . membership-groups from non-membership groups. These change with the changing situation. Vis-a-vis civilians . . . men in the Army may regard themselves and be regarded as members of an in-group; yet, in another context, enlisted men may regard themselves and be regarded as an in-group in distinction to the out-group of officers. Since these concepts are relative to the situation, rather than absolute, there is no paradox in referring to the officers as an out-group for enlisted men in one context, and as members of the more inclusive in-group in another context.[5]

The last sentence in the Merton-Kitt quotation, particularly, suggests the entirely symbolic character of membership; but at the same time the quotation illustrates how blunt an instrument is the membership-reference distinction for handling intricacies of group belonging. Another term, "multiple group membership," has also been coined to describe the evident fact that each of us belongs simultaneously to many groups. This term also reflects the layman's and the scientist's difficulties in assessing motivation. Since people do belong to many groups, a problem arises about any given situation: "as a member of which group is he acting now, or was he acting, or will he act?" This is, of course, simply another way of inquiring about situational identity.

"Multiple group membership," "reference group membership," judgments "anchored in group standards and frames of reference"—such terms come close to but do not directly focus on what, I would maintain, is the heart of membership: that is, its symbolic character. When we participate in cooperative activities we learn, and develop, certain terminologies. Insofar as the perspectives of various groups are similar, we are able to participate simultaneously or successively in them without experiencing the need to reconcile conflicting terminologies. Some of these terminologies are, as a host of writers have observed, logically contradictory; yet we who act in accordance with them may not be aware of our inconsistency. A man may purchase a "modern home," having developed his architectural tastes through discussions with artists, other modern art enthusiasts, and his reading of magazines; but may expect his wife to cook the foods he and she learned to like while living in slum tenements as members of immigrant families. Different standards apply to home and food consumption. House buying and home living, in fact, are not widely regarded as consumption. In similar vein, sociologists sometimes use the example of a man acting as a Christian on Sunday and a businessman on Monday, and they note that many men seem to be able to "disassociate" or keep in watertight compartments the different "role demands." To ask whether someone is more an immigrant than a member of the *avant garde,* or whether he is more a businessman than a Christian, is to raise pointless questions. When a man buys a modern house, he is acting as would others who share his terminology of perception and judgment. When he tells his wife not to experiment with the "American" recipes that stud the same magazines from whence he derived some of his best architectural ideas, then he is acting as do others who share his discriminations in food.

The members of any group necessarily experience certain areas of conceptual disagreement as well as non-communication. Groups are composed of individuals who, after all, bring with them to their participation in cooperative activity a body of symbolization derived from their other memberships. These symbols brought to the group from the outside contribute to the inevitable formation of subgroups, as for instance cliques among school teachers or those characteristic groupings of family quarrels that form along sex and age lines. Just because there exists within any group a divergency of concepts (whether imported or developed) there is frequent, not to say continual, formation and dissolution of coalitions, splinter groups, cliques, and other sub-groupings. Symbols, we may conclude, are pregnant with possibilities for convergence and divergence, for combination and permutation. Meanings, to quote John Dewey again, "breed new meanings."

Concepts, Coordinate Action, and Abstract Groupings

There are further intricacies of membership, and hence of identity, that can be hypothesized if we take seriously the theme that group life is organized around communication. Five decades ago the German sociologist, Georg Simmel, discussed this very point, and some of his discussion is helpful for extending our own. I begin this section with his analysis because it is easily comprehended, and is perhaps less contestable than what I shall say thereafter.

Simmel raised a question of the different "criteria" that can be said to underlie the organization of certain groups. By criteria he meant concepts: some groups are organized primarily around concepts having to do with kinship, others around concepts of age or sex, still others around something more abstract like scholarship or "emancipated womanhood" or "the solidarity of wage earners." Insofar as the conceptual bases of group organization vary, types of membership will vary. For instance:

Group formation during the Middle Ages was inspired by the idea that only equals could be associated, however often the practice deviated from the theory. . . . Hence, cities allied themselves first of all with cities, monasteries with monasteries, guilds with related guilds. This way of doing things was extended to alliances between different groups, but these groups were regarded even then as equal powers within the new alliance.[6]

These alliances did not involve their personnel in overlapping memberships but rather in inclusive ones. Hence, the problems posed for the individual were related to this association of equal groups. His problems necessarily were dissimilar to those of men who belong simultaneously to groups differently organized and associated. Medieval memberships were different than modern ones hence, as Simmel asserts, medieval men were different beings.

The historical question does not concern us, but the theoretical one does. The implication is that when people possess those concepts basic to the functioning of a particular organization, then they can participate in it. If they do not—if they are somewhat, or completely, out of conceptual range so to speak—what then? Of course, people who do not understand the purposes and the special languages of particular groups must learn these in order to participate: but there is a more profound sense in which outsiders may be beyond conceptual range.

Among those who are outside the boundaries of even ordinary public discourse are certain mental patients who suffer from impairment of thought processes (such as accompany aphasia and schizophrenia). It is said by some psychiatrists that these patients often cannot reason abstractly, or at least reason differently than before falling ill. Thus aphasics lose the ability to perform certain complex acts— to draw from memory, to classify an object, or to visualize themselves engaging in imaginary behavior—nevertheless, they can perform less complex acts such as drawing from a model or using objects without being able to classify them. The relevance of such impairment of action to participation in social groups is that participation often requires high "levels of thought": for instance, sustained attention, cogitation about absent objects, and choices among projected lines of future behavior.

Goldstein has suggested how drastically aphasia affected the intimate social relations of one of his cases. . . . Prior to his affliction he had been devoted to his family, but . . . during his stay at the hospital he appeared to show neither concern nor interest in his absent family. He became confused when any attempt was made to call his attention to them. A casual observer would have regarded him as callous and indifferent. Yet when he was sent to his home for brief visits he warmly displayed his former interest and devotion. Goldstein concludes that this patient's "out of sight, out of mind" attitude toward his wife and family grew directly out of his inability to formulate his relationships to his family when he was physically absent.[7]

We can similarly view children's deficiencies of conceptualization. There are countless social relationships into which young children cannot enter. This is true whether one asserts that they do not yet know enough or whether one asserts that they actually reason differently than adults. As he matures, each child is progressively able to enter (in any true sense) groups of greater, or more abstract, scope.

Granted that these limitations of conceptualization exist —in abnormals, subnormals, and in children—it may not be especially useful for us to phrase those limitations in terms of lower and higher modes of thought, or as is often said "concrete and abstract" reasoning. For us, the truly important limitation of the aphasic and the young child is their inability to enter into various types of group activity, totally or partially. Goldstein's patient can cooperate in family activity—when he is at home. The young child can buy groceries at the store—but not with any genuine comprehension of profit and monetary exchange.

Something akin to this is suggested if you will assume that different populations conceptualize somewhat differently, and therefore can cooperate only in limited or in special ways. For instance, psychiatrists frequently find it difficult to retain clinical patients who are of the "lower class." Probably more is involved than mere suspicion of the physician's strange manners, for as Meyers and Shaffer suggest, "lower class persons do not seem to share with psychiatrists the conception of therapy as a process by which the patient gains insight into his problems."[8] When such a patient conceives of the psychiatrist as "doing good for me," he is cooperating in ways that are probably different than those of well-educated patients who can better understand psychiatric perspectives.

Undoubtedly, different conceptions of what communication is, what conversation is, and what information is, are held by different populations. These conceptions condition the ways, and extent, that these populations can communicate with each other. Again I draw an example from the area of social class, this time from my own research. After a tornado had swept through a small town, its citizens were asked to tell about the storm and their experiences of it. The interviewers were middle class; the townspeople (measured by income and education) were both middle class and lower class. The modes of communication of the two classes proved to be quite dissimilar. Middle class people organized their accounts carefully, keeping the listener in mind, orienting him regarding time, place, and kind of event, and they fashioned their accounts according to some guiding conception of what had happened. The lower class people, apparently unused to communicating with strangers about things that neither communicant takes for granted, told their stories in ways that were confusing to their listeners. They did not orient the outsider to names, places, and times; so that their stories were jumbled and he had to probe unmercifully to obtain adequate interviews. The middle class people generally regarded the interviewer as a representative of larger audiences (a governmental agency or an assembly of scientists, for instance), and the interview itself was viewed as helping victims of future tornadoes. The lower class person appeared to treat the interview more as a face-to-face conversation in which the other person was finding out something about the tornado. The interviewer was associated, in a blurred way, with people and organizations sent to the town from the outside "to help us"; but how conversation with the outsider was going to help things was less clear than to the middle class person who generally possesses a clearer conception of social structure and community institutions.[9] In sum: the modes of communication displayed by the middle and lower class respondents were dissimilar. Thus, the conceptualization of the interview, and perhaps of communication generally, greatly affects how and to what extent such populations can participate in common: in community and political action, for instance.

As the preceding examples illustrate, people can cooperate even when their conceptions of the cooperative act are quite different. A child can be examined by a doctor and believe it a game, and within certain limits, the difference of conceptualization makes no difference. On the other hand, for many cooperative actions it is convenient and indeed essential that the communicants share important concepts. Howard S. Becker, in a progress report of research on medical students, writes that physicians believe they can better diagnose certain diseases when their patients are well educated. It is possible that these patients are not merely more articulate but give a more orderly, hence more satisfactory, account of those symptoms which they judge relevant to the doctor's concerns. Part of the physician's job, at least in some medical specialties, is to teach patients how to report symptoms. When cooperative action between the physician and his patient extends over a long period of time, the physician doubtless will be found coaching the patient. An interesting reversal occurs when the latter knows more about his disease, in a way, than his physician. Renée Fox, who has studied chronically ill patients, reports that they are keen observers of the progression and meaning of their own symptoms, so that the doctors avowedly lean upon their proferred lay diagnoses or at least admit the patients to partnership in the official diagnosis.[10] Insofar as this occurs both parties are united in a strange kind of membership, with identities that could be phrased perhaps as "patient also doctor" and "doctor of a very special kind."

If group action is seen in this manner as communicative action then, in a sense, group formation can be related to the limits of communication. To paraphrase G. H. Mead,[11] those who share concepts thereby share the potential of "some time, some where," forming a group on the basis of these concepts. The sociologist, Louis Wirth, used to maintain that as long as certain men had something in common they could give birth to a group, providing they recognized what they had in common—and this could be literally anything, even red hair or an interest in Australian two pence stamps. We may go a step further and say, with Mead, that sometimes it is not even necessary that men recognize they hold things in common for group action to occur.

Conceived in this way, there are abstract groupings whose existence is not so apparent if one focuses primarily upon "common interests," "group structure," "defined statuses" and other such features of stable and readily discernible groups. A more appropriate model for conceiving the more elusive groupings might be that of a diffused and complex collective act into which numerous participants enter— whether or not they are aware of so doing. During the course of this collective act, as in any cooperative or coordinated action, things get done by the participants and things are done to the participants. A few remarks about the function of travel talk and travel imagery—both for tourists and for the places which receive them—may illustrate this not easily exemplified model of a highly abstract collective act. I am here, again, using a study of my own.[12]

The imagery that draws visitors to a metropolis for an enjoyable time is projected not only by tourist agencies but, in its less planned forms, by articles and pictures in the mass media and by the conversation of former visitors. This tourist imagery functions not only to attract the traveler but also to control him and his movements when he reaches the city. The metropolis is faced with an influx of strangers, sometimes in considerable number, who are temporarily free from the ordinary controls exerted by their home communities. Quite aside from whether or not the visitor will behave himself properly, it is necessary that social mechanisms exist to prevent his getting both himself and the natives into trouble. If he wanders into the wrong areas of town he might get hurt or robbed or killed or might witness untoward scenes, and so create awkward situations for those involved or for the city authorities. And an influential visitor might carry away and publicize facets of the city that would be injurious to its reputation. Also, it is not feasible to allow the tourist into industrial or business concerns except as members of guided tours. In short, the ordinary life of the city must go on, must not be unduly interfered with. The presence of strangers would be a problem unless they were confined—by force, rule or conception—to rather public sectors of the city.

Most tourists, most of the time, are on their own rather than on guided tours. They get into less trouble than they might because virtually all their activity occurs within a few of the most public sections of town. Much as the guide succeeds in routing his customers, the anticipatory imagery with which the tourist enters the city itself guides his steps. The tourist comes with a set of categories derived from his reading and conversation with those who have preceded him. He possesses prescriptions—however vague and unformulated—for seeing, seeking, walking, watching and feeling. These greatly restrict the many alternate modes of enjoying a particular city.

The conventional terms with which particular cities get described in travel talk constitute something like a "special language." The linguist, J. Vendreyes[13] has defined a special language as one "employed by groups of individuals placed in special circumstances." Every functioning group uses a lingo, a slang or specialized terminology. This terminology embodies and highlights matters of interest and import to its members. Tourists do not by any means constitute an organized group. Yet a coordinated, controlled, series of action goes on when tourists are attracted to a city and are routed directly, or indirectly, through it. We can readily single out some of the relevant functionaries (officials of tourist and travel agencies, guides, travel writers, catering restauranteurs, and sometimes taxi drivers). The goals, strategies, and skills requisite to this large scale collective act are also visible. But the act does not go on within a tightly knit social structure. The tourists themselves constitute something like what Herbert Blumer has called a "mass," with

no structure of status roles . . . no established leadership. It merely consists of an aggregate of individuals who are separate, detached, anonymous. . . . The form of mass behavior . . . is laid down by individual lines of action . . . in the form of selections.[14]

But individual lines of convergence—if not on California gold fields, then on Bermuda beaches or in glamorous cities —would appear to be part and parcel of an extended social act, coordinated in somewhat different fashion than the acts of tightly organized groups and institutions. Essential to this large scale act is a flow of communication, travel talk.

Whether or not you agree upon the usefulness of calling all this a collective act or some kind of abstract group, it is clear that all these acts of tourists, agents, agencies, and so on, are linked in anything but simple ways. A host of heterogeneous people have, through a multitude of shared concepts, been brought into a fluidly organized, great collective act. People have, to quote Dewey's phrase again, become "participants or parties in a conjoint undertaking"—one of great scope and abstraction. (Within this act there bubble up little acts, little groups—friendships, shipboard cliques, transitory traveling groups—that may or may not persist beyond the major act.) However difficult it may be to talk of memberships in such abstract groupings, and however transitory such memberships may be, they are immensely relevant to personal action and identity.

Easier to visualize perhaps, but equally neglected are those abstract groupings called in popular parlance "worlds": the world of drama, of art, fashion, crime, the radio, the homosexual, of baseball, and of medicine. These worlds always contain visible social structures—museums, radio stations— and are marked by much regularized behavior. Careers can be pursued within these worlds along fairly expectable lines.

But the central feature of social worlds is not their tightly knit nor extensive organization; just the opposite, for they are characterized by their looseness or diffuseness. Nevertheless the participants, and many outsiders, recognize types of participants in these worlds and various types of events that take place there.

Tomatsu Shibutani has called our attention to the dependence of these networks of participants upon channels of communication. Worlds, he writes, are essentially shared perspectives. His analysis of communication as it relates to social worlds is so similar to my preceding discussion that I cannot forbear quoting at length from his analysis.

As Dewey emphasized, society exists in and through communication; common perspectives—common cultures—emerge through participation in common communication channels. It is through social participation that perspectives shared in a group are internalized. . . .

Modern mass societies . . . are made up of a bewildering variety of social worlds. Each is an organized outlook, built up by people in their interaction with one another; here, each communication channel gives rise to a separate world. . . . Each is an area in which there is some structure which permits reasonable anticipation of the behavior of others. . . . Each social world . . . is a culture area, the boundaries of which are set neither by territory nor by formal group membership but by the limits of effective communication.

Since there is a variety of communication channels, differing in stability and extent, social worlds differ in composition, size, and the territorial distribution of the participants. . . . Worlds differ in the extent and clarity of their boundaries; each is confined by some kind of horizon, but this may be wide or narrow, clear or vague. . . . Most important of all, social worlds are not static entities; shared perspectives are continually being reconstituted.[15]

Shibutani goes on to say that because people belong to many and different social worlds, it is important to know "the social world in which he is participating in a given act." In short: the problem of membership is complicated by participation in these extremely real but elusive groups, titled for want of a better term "worlds."

When we begin to discuss not merely the worlds themselves but their members, we pile complexity upon complexity. Even a fairly well structured and very visible world, such as the world of medicine, raises fabulously difficult problems of identity: for the members themselves, and for those social scientists who wish to study medical identities. Questions are raised similar to those asked in the preceding section about race and religion. Who is more a physician: one who has patients, or one who has none? Some physicians have as clients only other physicians. Some doctors are attacked by their colleagues as mere technicians and must develop strategies to counter the accusation. Likewise those who do little more than converse with their patients (certain psychiatrists) must develop rituals and signs of identification to link them with the profession at large. As medical techniques evolve, as equipment is invented, as the human body becomes more fully understood, new medical specialties then develop and old ones split into several or disappear entirely. The new specialists must exert their claims, sometimes upon strange grounds, that what they are doing is medicine and that they too are physicians. The old-fashioned doctor as he becomes a bit outmoded must wrestle with problems of what, really, "is" a doctor. Above and behind the cloud of disputation and rhetoric lie vague general notions of "medicine" and of "the physician." Perhaps these very general or abstract concepts are all that keep "the profession" together; and perhaps the medical school has as its major function the inculcation of these and the accompanying generalized medical identity. Some social worlds, as Shibutani notes, have more diffuse boundaries than medicine does; hence have much less rigorous tests of recruitment; yet one is struck by similar problems of belonging and identity. Membership within all these social worlds involves

various generalized commitments, beyond the more specific
and easily discernible commitments, to agencies, institutions,
organizations, cliques, and specialties associated with the
social world.

History: Heritage, Memorialization, and Creation

As I remarked near the end of the last chapter, one ought
not to speak of group membership without painstakingly
seeking to take history into account. Identities imply not
merely personal histories but also social histories. The preceding statement follows rather simply from this: individuals
hold memberships in groups that themselves are products of
a past. If you wish to understand persons—their development
and their relations with significant others—you must be prepared to view them as embedded in historical context. Psychological and psychiatric theory, at least of the American variety,
underplay this context; and those sociologists and anthropologists who are interested in personal identity tend to
treat historical matters more as stage settings, or backdrops,
than as crucial to the study of persons. This is an oversimpli-
fication, I am certain, of the use and lack of use that is
made of historical materials in social psychology. Nevertheless it allows me to state forthrightly a view of history that is
implicit throughout this essay.

A man must be viewed as embedded in a temporal matrix
not simply of his own making, but which is peculiarly and
subtly related to something of his own making—his conception of the past as it impinges on himself. I take the liberty
here of using some autobiographical comments by Sir Osbert
Sitwell to make this proposition especially vivid. Do not be
deceived by these comments: they are unusual merely because
Sir Osbert belongs to an aristocratic world and thereby seems

incredibly affected by his sense of an impinging and lively past.

The first volume of his autobiography bears the title of *Left Hand, Right Hand*[16] which Sir Osbert is at pains to explain is "because, according to the palmists, the lines of the left hand are incised inalterably at birth, while those of the right hand are modified by our actions and environment, and the life we lead." The left hand theme is encountered on the initial pages, which portray his father walking over the ancestral grounds, upon or near which the family has lived for seven centuries. For his father the Middle Ages "are the model for all life to follow, and his life was largely devoted to living out that model." Like others of the British aristocracy at the turn of the century "he was interested more in ancestors and descendants than in sons and fathers." During a walk—the book opens with a description of it—the father remarks to Osbert, "It's quite evident, if you read the family letters, that we've been working up toward something for a long time, for well over a century." He did not mean, and did not realize, that three of his children were to become recognized as among Great Britain's most celebrated writers; but Sir Osbert himself is concerned, in the autobiography, with the very questtion of how this was to come about.

Who knows whence come the various traits of sensibility? Ancestors stretch behind a man and his nature like a fan, or the spread tail of a peacock. At every turn, in the very gesture and look, in every decision he takes, he draws on the reserves or deficits of the past.

Naturally he has countless ancestors. He makes no claim that all are important to his own character and personal history: but he has taken the trouble to record, through some seventy pages, fact and anecdote about various of his father's and mother's ancestors. They may possibly be relevant to his

autobiography. What is more, it is apparent that Sir Osbert
is versed in their lives. Aristocratic families leave records,
letters, and diaries to their descendants, and appear on the
pages and in the memoirs of contemporary authors and
acquaintances. Sir Osbert knows his many ancestors as others
know their immediate relatives. He is writing with restraint:
he could write volumes about his kin. Once through these
introductory pages, and unleashed upon the actual story of
his life, Sir Osbert brings into his narrative his living kin;
displaying a keen sense of what was happening to them,
during the specific period that he, as a youth, was meeting
and experiencing them. Personal relations are hardly ever
described merely as personal, they are embroidered into an
historic tapestry. In his own words: he is writing of his elders
and of "people who died before I was born, but who still
influence me, perhaps, in ways I do not know as well as in
ways to be recognized."

You may exclaim that this is a very particular kind of
memory, valued and possessed only by certain kinds of people
and populations. This is not the point. Even when a man
lacks knowledge of kinship history, this has bearing upon the
fact and sense of his identity: to his name both in the literal
sense and in the reputational sense. America was settled by
immigrants who thereby cut off their children from extensive
memories; memory stopping, so to speak, at our shores and
reaching no further back than the ancestor who migrated.
The discrepancy between the sons of migrants and those
inheritors of longer American genealogies—with heirlooms,
histories, and prestige to match—is still noticeable on the
American scene. The attempts to maintain, repudiate and
acquire such symbolic genealogies are, as is well known, important endeavors of some of our citizens. Kinship is so
entwined with social class that a deficiency of kinship memories means also deficiency of class memories. American
fiction and autobiography have recorded the quashing of old

class memories by upwardly mobile persons, and the some-times frantic acquisition of historical and anecdotal knowl-edge of the social class into which they are moving.

But the impact of history upon identity involves much more than consciousness of kinship and placement in a social class. Harking back to a previous discussion of "present, past, and future" in the second chapter, it seems unnecessary to belabor this point; although it will pay to note two further aspects of the relation between history and personal identity. The first is this: a people may create an historical past which they do not possess, or discard a past and then create a new one. Thus, in the development of nationalistic movements, and in the nationalism of nations, the past may be recreated in the image of the desired present and future. Many his-torians have documented, Carleton Hayes among them,[17] that these imagined and glorious pasts are laboriously and care-fully created through the various mass media. This has led George Orwell to depict the ultimate in totalitarian control, in his reverse Utopia, *Nineteen Eighty-Four*,[18] where history was completely rewritten through the creation of "newspeak," a special language which permitted only certain limited ideas to be conceived. E. C. Hughes[19] has written of another na-tionalistic tendency: he suggests that under conditions of tribal disintegration as in Africa, when nationalistic move-ments form, they and the countries which emerge from them must quite literally create new mythical national histories. They must do this in order that their heterogeneous popula-tions be brought together under one banner. Thus the emerg-ing territorial boundaries, and the emerging collective acts, will be rationalized in terms of a symbolic past as well as a realistic present.

This leads me to a second point that actually none of this is very different than occurs in the more humdrum histories of less dramatically changing groups and organizations. Each generation perceives the past in new terms, and rewrites its own history. Insofar as there are shared group-perspectives bearing upon the past, the selves of the component members are vitally affected. Certain groups and organizations have immensely long histories, and strong vested interests, in preserving and reviewing their histories. An American thinks immediately of the South since the Civil War. Even the writings of professional historians, white and Negro, are a reflection of each generation's successively revised posture toward the past and a contribution toward what is known and felt about that past.

In Europe, collective memories are longer, and so identities may be linked with conceptions of ancient eras. The citizens of Nuremberg have an urban history which includes a glorious sixteenth century. The signs of it are visible in the churches, in the houses, in the very street plan of the central city; so that when the center of the city was badly destroyed during the war, little or no question was raised afterwards whether it should be reconstructed in modern styles. It was deliberately rebuilt to recapture, if possible, something of the atmosphere of the past, and ancient public buildings were sometimes rebuilt from the ground up at great cost. This is not to say that the identities of all citizens of Nuremburg are equally involved with the city's past, nor in the same ways: but Nuremberg's past hovers over the city visibly, gets into the press and into conversation; and must be taken into account even by those who spurn or fight it. Nuremburg's bustling business men have recently published a book about their city, advertising its great industrial capacity and potential. They necessarily had to couch their slogans in opposition to the city's past, for even the outside world thinks of Nuremburg first and foremost as a treasure house of German medieval art, rather than as a progressive industrial city. "We are happy to present at this time a city in the bloom of a new youth. Its title [the book] might well be 'Nuremburg the living city.' "[20]

A Case History: Collective Memory and Personal Identity

The relation of personal identity to public history being what it is, there is a moral to be drawn for those of us who wish to study personal identity. Persons can be conceived as taking some particular stance toward the historical, suprapersonal, past. They will be memorializing it, rejecting it, recreating it, cashing in on it, escaping, or in flight from it; these are but a few of countless possibilities. Personal styles are built around such possibilities, and entire series of personal acts may be viewed as strategies in rejecting, escaping, recapturing, and the like. A man may write a book, marry a woman, or build an organization for such ends. When we interview persons we catch them during some temporal cross-section in the building or transforming of styles that link to history: this is one important way to regard the contents of interviews and conversations.

As an exercise in the analysis of such styles, I offer a case study consisting of an extended quotation from Rebecca West's magnificently sensitive report on Yugoslavia, published in 1940. Hitherto, I have not used long blocks of quoted material, but here the device should be useful. The "case" will be presented first, and the analysis or commentary will follow.

There is no end to political disputation in Croatia. None. . . . They had quarrelled all through lunch. We had spent the morning going round the sights of the town with a Croat lady and Constantine, and over the soup we told Valetta how much we had liked her; and Constantine had exploded: "I did not like her. She is not a true Slav. Did you hear what she told you when you were at the Health Co-operative Society Clinic? She said that all such things were very well looked after in the Austrian times. Yes, and she said it regretfully." "Well, it was so," said Valetta. "Yes, it was so," said Constantine, "but we must not regret it. No true Slav would regret it. That is to say no true human being would say it, for a true human being is a Slav, he knows that to be a Slav is what is important, for that is the shape which God has given him, and he should keep it. The Austrians sometimes pampered you, and sometimes the Hungarians, so that each should play you off against the others. Benefits you get so are filth, and they spoil your shape as a Slav. It is better to have nearly nothing at all, and be a freeman with your brother Slavs." He paused, but Valetta was silent and went on eating. "Do you not think it is better?" Constantine asked him. He nodded slightly. "Well, if you do not feel that strongly you can feel nothing at all!" said Constantine a little louder. "Oh, yes, I feel it strongly," said Valetta, quite softly, and then, more softly still, "It would be much better for us to be freeman with our brother Slavs."

For a moment Constantine was satisfied and went on eating. Then he threw down his knife and fork. "What is it that you are saying? It *would* be better. . . . You mean it is not so?" "I mean it is not quite so," said Valetta. "How is it not so?" asked Constantine, lowering his head like a bull. Valetta shrugged his shoulders. Constantine collapsed quite suddenly, and asked pathetically, "But we are not brothers, we Croats and Serbs?" "Yes," said Valetta. He was speaking softly . . . out of intense feeling. He was quite white. "But in Yugoslavia . . . it is not so. Or, rather, it is as if the Serbs were the elder brother and we Croats the younger brother, under some law . . . which gives the older everything and the younger nothing." "Oh, I know what you think!" groaned Constantine. "You think that all your money goes to Belgrade, and you get hardly anything of it back, and we flood your country with Serb officials, and keep Croats out of all positions of real power. I know it all!"

"You may know it all!" said Valetta, "but so do we: and it is not a thing we can be expected to overlook." "I do not ask you to overlook it," said Constantine, beginning to roar like a bull, "I ask you to look at it. You did not have the spending of your money before, when you were under Hungary. All your money was sent to Budapest to landlords or to tax-collectors, and you got some railways, yes, and some hospitals, yes, and some roads, yes, but not costing one-half of your money, and you got also Germanization and Magyarization, you got the violation of your soul. But now you are part of Yugoslavia, you are a part of the kingdom of the South Slavs, which exists to let you keep your soul, and to guard that kingdom we must have an army and a navy . . . and we must give Serbia many things she did not have because Serbia was fighting the Turk when you were standing safe behind us, and we must do much for Bosnia, because the Hungarians did nothing there, and we must do everything for Macedonia, because the Turks were there 'til 1912, and we must drain marshes and build schools and make military roads, and it is all for you as well as for us, but you will not see it."

"Yes, I see it," said Valetta, "but if you want to found a strong and civilized Yugoslavia you should have brought the Serb schools up to the Croat level instead of bringing the Croat schools down to Serb level." "But now you should see nothing at all," wailed Constantine; "it is a question of money. It is more important that one should have good schools everywhere than that part of the country should have very good schools. A chain is as strong as its weakest link. What good is it to you in Croatia that your boys and girls can read the Hindustani and paint like Raphael if the young men in Macedonia go bang-bang all night at whoever because they do not know anything else to do?" "We might feel more confidence that our money went to build schools in Macedonia if it did not go through Belgrade. . . . You must forgive us for fearing that a great deal of it sticks in Belgrade." "Of course it sticks in Belgrade!" said Constantine, his voice going high, though it is low by nature. "We must make a capital. We must make a capital for your sake, because you are a South Slav! All Western Europeans despise us because we have a little capital that is not chic. They are wrong, for there is no reason why we should have a big capital, for we are a peasant state. But you must give these people what they want . . . it is a big shining thing that impresses them. Do you not remember how before the war the Austrian Ministers treated us like dirt, because Vienna is a place of baroque palaces and we had nothing but our poor town. . . ."

". . . why do you not draw on us Croats for officials?" asked Valetta. ". . . But how can we let you Croats be officials?" spluttered Constantine. "You are not loyal!" "And how," asked Valetta, white to the lips, "can we be expected to be loyal if you always treat us like this?" "But I am telling you," grieved Constantine, "how can we treat you differently 'til you are loyal?"

It is an absolute deadlock; and the statement of it filled the heart with desolation. Constantine pushed away his plate and said, "Valetta, I will tell you what is the matter with you. . . . Here in Croatia you are lawyers as well as soldiers. You have been good lawyers, and you have been lawyers all the time. For eight hundred years you have had your *procès* against Hungary. You have quibbled over phrases in the *diploma inaugurale* of your kings, you have wrangled about the power of your Ban, you have sawed arguments about *regna socia* and *partes adnexae*, you have chattered like jackdaws over your rights under the Dual Monarchy, you have covered acres of paper discussing the Hungaro-Croatian compromise. And so it is that you are now more lawyers than soldiers, for it is not since the eighteenth century that you have fought the Turks. . . . But now we are making Yugoslavia we must feel not like lawyers but like soldiers. . . . You must cast away all your little rights, and say that we have a big right, the right of the Slavs to be together, and we must sacrifice all our rights to protect the great right."

Valetta shrugged his shoulders once more. "What have you against that?" roared Constantine. "I will tell you what is the matter with you. You are an intellectual, you are all intellectuals here in the bad sense. You boast because Zagreb is an old town, but that is a great pity for you. Everywhere else in Serbia is a new town, and though we have novelists and poets and all, they have now been in no town not more than . . . one generation. . . . So what the peasant knows they also know. They know that one must not work against, one must work with. . . . But in the town you do not know that, you can go through life and you can work against all. . . . So you are intellectuals. The false sort that are always in opposition. My God, my God, how easy it is to be an intellectual in opposition to the man of action! He can always be so much cleverer, he can always pick out the little faults. But to make, that is more difficult . . . *Ach*, in all your little ways you are very terrible!"

For a time Valetta did not answer. . . . "You would say we are well governed here?" he asked presently. "You would say that nobody is arrested without cause and thrown into prison and treated barbarously? You would say that nobody has been tortured in Croatia since it became Yugoslavia?" He was trembling, and such sick horror passed across his face that I am sure he was recollecting atrocities which he had seen with his own eyes, at which his own bowels had revolted. Constantine nearly cried. "Ah, God! it is their fault," he pled, indicating my husband and myself. "These English are hypocrites, they pretend they govern people without using force, because there are many parts of the Empire where they govern only people who want to be governed . . . in India where the people do not want to be governed many people are beaten and imprisoned. And for that I do not blame the English. It must be done if one race has to have power over another; that is why it is wrong for one race to have power over another, and that is why we must have a Yugoslavia, a self-governing kingdom of the South Slavs, and why we should make all possible sacrifices for Yugoslavia." "I see the argument," said Valetta; "we are to let Serbs torture us Croats, because under Yugoslavia we are not to be tortured by the Italians and Hungarians." "Oh, God. Oh, God!" cried Constantine, "I am glad that I am not a Croat, but a Serb, for though I myself am a very clever man, the Serbs are not a very clever people; that has not been their business; their business has been to drive out the Turks and keep their independence from the Austrians and the Germans . . . my God, my God, do you know what I feel like doing when I talk to you Croats? I feel like rolling up my coat and lying down in the middle of the street and putting my head on my coat, and saying to the horses and motor cars, 'Drive on, I am disgusted.' What is so horrible in this conversation is that you are never wrong, but I am always right, and we could go on talking like this for ever, till the clever way you are never wrong brought death upon us." "Some have died already," said Valetta.[21]

I wish to use this passionate debate for only one purpose: to make the point unforgettably that personal identity is meshed with group identity, which itself rests upon an historical past. The Croatian looks back across the centuries and sees the oppression of his people, and of the Slavs in general; and now sees a continuation of this oppression by one of the Slav peoples. If anything, the current oppression is a worst form, hence his confrontation of the Serb with accusations of betrayal. Valetta, the Croat, rises to his strongest pitches of anger and revulsion when he insinuates or hurls these accusations, and especially when Constantine paradoxically accuses the Croations of disloyalty to all Slavs. To

Valetta, Yugoslavia ought to mean freedom; but freedom cannot signify merely being free from the Austrians, the Hungarians, and the Turks; it must mean a true lack of oppression by anyone. We may hazard, also, that since Valetta believes the Croats represent a high point of civilization, he also believes Croatians ought to be the true leaders of the Slavs. Real freedom cannot be gained at the expense of loss of those civilizational values. These latter are not merely "education" and "schooling" but as Constantine himself suggests constitute dear possessions, deeply rooted in the Croatians' conception of themselves.

Constantine's identity is equally linked with the centuries, but if anything appears more complex because the Serbs had changed from an age-old status ("oppressed by non-Slavs") through another ("leaders of the victory over the outsiders") to the current one ("rulers in cooperation with fellow Slavs"). Victory in the battle for freedom justifies the Serb as a man of action, for the highest goal was freedom from oppression. Previous concessions wrung from the oppressors, by legal means, are forgotten or not recognized by Constantine; history is perceived as leading up to the final great right, the right for all Slavs to be free together. Those who are, so to speak, handed their freedom, who never really earned it, should at least cooperate in building a great Slavic country. At this juncture of history, the important thing is to forget specific identities and be a "true Slav." They are all born Slavs, but the essence of the true Slavic identity is that it is earned. The Serbs earned theirs by winning the victory, and by working toward a great and united Yugoslavia. In a certain sense, Constantine regards the Croats as traitors: they have not been instrumental in winning the victory; they are not cooperating now that victory is won; and they are all the more culpable because they are the best educated of all Slavic people. (Constantine himself is a poet and an intellectual.) At the same time, we might guess, the stress placed upon the Serb as a man of action could not be so pronounced if the legalistic Croat did not exist as a vivid and exasperating contrast. Constantine's vulnerability—the dilemma confronting him—is that he is now one of the rulers whereas all his life has been styled as, and has styled himself as, one of the oppressed. The transition has left him open to charges of treachery, of being no different than the Austrians—except infinitely worse, because he is a Slav. Such accusations strike at the roots of his being, for he and the Serbs are the defenders and the liberators of all Slavs. Slavs have not been free for centuries but now they are. Rebecca West has probably caught accurately Constantine's moments of greatest anguish and fury when he is accused of betrayal. His sensitivity to the problems of British rule, and to the images of backwardness held of Yugoslavia by wealthier countries, is part of his transition from oppressed to ruler. This is a transition unquestionably fraught with anxiety. The Serbian history of oppression does not yield many cues for handling this unaccustomed new status. Perhaps the rule of the British does?

Against this analysis, and against the case study itself, it may be protested that the dice—again—have been loaded, that this long quotation shows men who are embedded passionately in group histories but that most men are not. The reply is as before: this is not the point. This kind of material merely highlights what one ought to look for in men whose lives are not so obviously enmeshed in long group histories. Then the analysis becomes more difficult and possibly more subtle. A social psychology without full focus upon history is a blind psychology. A concern with personal styles, strategies, careers—in short, with personal identities—requires a serious parallel concern with shared, or collective identities, viewed through time.

If you take seriously my contention, then you must agree that new kinds of technical training and innovation are re-

quired. Social psychologists and sociologists are not usually
trained in historical method (indeed are generally suspicious
of it except within its own "proper" domain) nor do they
traditionally think, as does the historian, in terms of long
temporal spans. Social psychologists, especially, typically
study short sequences of action; or at most, the duration of
single life cycles. Yet historians, as R. Richard Wohl has
pointed out,[22] are neither seriously interested in many of the
problems touched upon in this essay nor are they particularly
equipped with concepts for grappling with these problems.
What seems called for, to supplement the methods and training now current, is something of the frame of reference of
the historian, along with his professional training in piecing
together evidence from documents; but with this, attitude
and skill oriented toward particular kinds of theoretical
problems. Those of us who have worked with unstandardized
interviews, life histories, and piecemeal observations should
not find the historian's skills and perspective at variance
with our own; for field methods merely rely less on library
documents and have a shorter temporal focus. The same kind
of ingenuity in piecing together somewhat scattered and
non-comparable bits of evidence to give composite proof is
the hallmark of both trades. With some audacity on our part,
we may even legitimately do original research with wholly
non-contemporary materials, the whole endeavor being cen-
tered around our abiding interest in personal and collective
identity.

CHAPTER SEVEN

A Concluding Note

IN THIS ESSAY I have attempted to bring together an emphasis upon symbolic behavior and another emphasis upon social organization—and by doing so to suggest a fruitful, systematic, perspective from which the traditional problems of social psychology might be viewed. (My emphasis upon the historical dimension is subsidiary, although necessary as counterweight to its disregard by social psychologists.) The essay is shorter than it could be, for I have purposely left out dozens of topics that might have been covered. My intent was not to be exhaustive but to open up, if possible, vistas and to relate together matters not ordinarily thought of as so connected. I have had in mind constantly that psychiatrists and psychologists underestimate immensely the influence of social organization upon individual behavior and individual structure; and conversely that sociologists, whose major concern is with social organization, must in much of their research depend upon some kind of social psychology.

That kind of association between sociology and social psychology began, in this country, as far back as the 1890's when sociologists first had broken loose from political science and history, and were seeking general laws of societal and group behavior. They shortly began to perceive that to study groups and societies, they ought also to study "the psychological side of society." This tradition of conceiving of a social psychology as indispensable to, and only analytically separable from sociology comes down unbroken through the years. I can illus-

trate this point by quoting Talcott Parsons, who writes in a
volume devoted to "convergence" in anthropology, psychology and sociology that "the basic problem of this paper . . .
is, from the sociological point of view, to state some of the
most essential requirements of a psychological theory which
is maximally useful to the sociologist."[1] True to his purpose,
he has attempted in this paper to assess current psychological
theories as they have bearing upon the problems in which he,
as a sociologist, is interested. Parsons does with full consciousness (here, and in other well known writings) what many
sociologists, it seems to me, do more implicitly; that is, to
draw upon some sort of a social psychology for cues, hints,
and interpretations concerning those aspects of their own
work that appear to them to require psychological under-
pinning. This dependence of the sociologist upon a social
psychology—whether that dependence is declared or is covert
—was once nicely stated to me by a colleague, Peter Blau, the
author of a study of bureaucritic organization[2] (in which
implicit use was made of psychological terms). Blau remarked
that students of social organization, like himself, in order
to work out a fruitful theory of social organization will have
to develop its social psychological aspects, or will have to
draw upon the theoretical statements of social psychologists.
Naturally, he added, it would be more convenient to have a
fruitful social psychology available. The moot question, of
course, is just what kind of a social psychology? Will it be
one that is based primarily upon learning theory? Upon
psychoanalytic propositions? Upon exhaustive experimenta-
tion with small groups? Upon a wedding of a symbolic perspective with studies of social organization? In any case, a
systematic social psychology is a necessity to sociology and is
(and has been) less a field or a specialty within sociology
than a pervasive stance.

The situation has been quite otherwise within the field of

psychology, where social psychology (and the study of personality too) has had to fight an uphill battle for legitimacy and prestige; and where the dominant perspective has always been upon problems of individual behavior and individual organization. Despite the fruitful contact of psychology with sociology and anthropology during the last two decades, it seems probable that most social psychologists who have trained in psychology departments are more closely linked with learning theory and clinical theory than intellectual movements in allied sciences. (Is it a nostalgic connection, or a sense of vivid identity, which makes these social psychologists direct certain of their remarks at their colleagues? To an outsider, there is something of the missionary about these remarks. But if the social psychologists' commitments to psychology are deep, as it appears to me they are, then the crusading spirit is comprehensible—part and parcel of the effort whereby they make social psychology an eminent specialty within psychology proper.) Psychiatry, of course, has its roots deep in medical science, both historically and, to a great extent, currently. Its focus is still upon maladjusted individuals. Only lately has it come to encompass, in some of the work of its practitioners, some interest in social factors that may affect mental health and its treatment.

It is unlikely that the general fields of psychology and psychiatry will change their traditional foci or abandon cherished assumptions anymore than one would expect sociologists and anthropologists to yield their preoccupation with social organization and culture. Yet in those interstitial areas lying between the major disciplines, within which social psychology seems to fall, the problems of identity with which I have dealt are of immense concern. I have tried my hand in this essay at pulling together certain approaches to those problems. It would be a feat worthy of our generation of scholarship if someone could fuse—not merely juxtapose

References

Preface

1. Erik H. Erikson, "The Problem of Identity," *Journal of American Psychoanalysis*, IV (1956), 56-121.

Chapter I

1. Carson McCullers, *The Member of the Wedding* (New York: New Directions, 1951), pp. 13, 25-27.
2. Kenneth Burke, *A Grammar of Motives* (New York: Prentice-Hall, 1945), p. 24.
3. John Dewey, *Reconstruction in Philosophy* (New York: Henry Holt, 1920), p. 86.
4. John Dewey, *Experience and Nature* (Chicago: Open Court, 1925), p. 399.
5. George H. Mead, *Mind, Self and Society* (Chicago: University of Chicago Press, 1934).
6. Kenneth Burke, *op. cit.*, p. xix.
7. *Ibid.*, p. 19.
8. *Ibid.*, p. 25.

Chapter II

1. Mead, *op. cit.*, p. 174.
2. Gilbert Ryle, *The Concept of Mind* (New York: Barnes and Noble, 1950), p. 195.
3. *Ibid.*, p. 196.
4. Kurt Riezler, *Man: Mutable and Immutable* (Chicago: Regnery, 1950), p. 80.

181

5. *Ibid.*, p. 78.

6. George H. Mead, *Movements of Thought in the Nineteenth Century* (Chicago: University of Chicago Press, 1936), p. 69.

7. Charles H. Cooley, *Human Nature and the Social Order* (Glencoe: The Free Press, 1956), p. 184.

8. Gustavus A. Cunningham, *A Study in the Philosophy of Bergson* (New York: Longmans, Green, 1916).

9. Albert Camus, "Art in Revolt," *Partisan Review*, 1952, p. 274.

10. Helmut Kuhn, *Encounter with Nothingness* (London: Methuen, 1951), p. 25.

11. *Loc. cit.*

12. John Dewey, *Human Nature and Conduct* (New York: Henry Holt, 1922), pp. 216-17.

Chapter III

1. George H. Mead, *Mind, Self and Society;* Burke, *op. cit.,* and *Permanence and Change* (New York: New Republic, 1936); C. Wright Mills, "Situated Actions and Vocabularies of Motive," *American Sociological Review*, V (1940), 904-13; Hans Gerth and C. Wright Mills, *Character and Social Structure* (Boston: Harcourt Brace, 1953); Alfred Lindesmith and Anselm Strauss, *Social Psychology* (2nd ed.; New York: Dryden, 1956); Nelson Foote, "Identification as the Basis for a Theory of Motivation," *American Sociological Review*, XVI (1951), 14-22.

2. Foote, *op. cit.,* p. 18.

3. Mills, *op. cit.,* p. 906.

4. The study referred to is directed by E. C. Hughes. His associates are Howard Becker, Blanche Geer, David Riesman and myself, working in conjunction with the University of Kansas Medical School and Community Studies, Inc., of Kansas City, Missouri.

5. *Ibid.*

6. Foote, *op. cit.,* p. 15.

7. Lindesmith and Strauss, *Social Psychology* (New York: Dryden, 1949), p. 312.

8. Mills, *op. cit.,* p. 907.

9. Alfred H. Stanton and Morris S. Schwartz, *The Mental Hospital* (New York: Basic Books, 1954), pp. 200, 203, 205-06.

10. Ralph H. Turner, "Role-Taking, Role Standpoint, and Reference-Group Behavior," *American Journal of Sociology*, LXI (1956), 316-28.

11. Since these lines were written, I have had the opportunity to read some materials by Gregory P. Stone of the University of Missouri who, in a study of women's clothes, has found it useful to distinguish among appraisals of value, mood, and anticipated behavior. (These can be appraisals of one's own behavior as well as that of others.)

12. Herbert Blumer, "Psychological Import of the Human Group," in M. Sherif and M. Wilson (eds.), *Social Relations at the Crossroads* (New York: Harper, 1953), p. 95.

13. *Ibid.*

14. Robert Faris, *Social Psychology* (New York: Ronald, 1952), p. 100.
15. Suzanne K. Langer, *Philosophy in a New Key* (Cambridge, Mass.: Harvard University Press, 1942).
16. *Op. Cit.* (1956 ed.), p. 209.
17. This research, at the University of Chicago, has not yet been published.
18. Harry S. Sullivan, *Conceptions of Modern Psychiatry* (Washington: W. A. White Psychiatric Foundation, 1947), p. 45.
19. Neal Gross and W. S. Mason, "Some Methodological Problems of Eight Hour Interviews," *American Journal of Sociology*, LIX (1953), 197-204.
20. Everett C. Hughes, "Dilemmas and Contradictions of Status," *American Journal of Sociology*, L (1945), 353-59.
21. Cf. Richard H. Williams, "Scheler's Contributions to the Sociology of Affective Action, with Special Attention to the Problem of Shame," *Philosophy and Phenomenological Research*, II (1942).
22. Erving Goffman, "Communication Conduct in an Island Community," Ph.D. Thesis, University of Chicago, Department of Sociology, 1953.
23. Harold Garfinkel, "Conditions of Successful Degradation Ceremonies," *American Journal of Sociology*, LXI (1956), 432.
24. Orrin E. Klapp, "The Fool as a Social Type," *American Journal of Sociology*, LV (1949), 159-60.
25. Talcott Parsons, *The Social System* (Glencoe: The Free Press, 1951), pp. 439-54.
26. Erving Goffman, "On Face-Work, An Analysis of Ritual Elements in Social Interaction," *Psychiatry*, XVIII (1955), 213-31.
27. *Op. cit.*, pp. 160-61.
28. Lindesmith and Strauss, *op. cit.* (1956 ed.), p. 528.
29. Cf. M. Schwartz, "Patient Demands in a Mental Hospital Context," *Psychiatry*, XX (1957), 249-61.

Chapter IV

1. Horace Kallen, *Patterns of Progress* (New York: Columbia University Press, 1950), p. 26.
2. *Ibid.*, p. 72.
3. Robert Potter, "A Working Paper for the Sociability Project" (Under the direction of David Riesman and Jeanne Watson, University of Chicago, 1956).
4. A similar but more elaborate treatment of this subject can be found in Howard S. Becker and Anselm Strauss, "Careers, Personality and Adult Socialization," *American Journal of Sociology*, November, 1956.
5. Robert K. Merton, *Social Structure and Social Theory* (Glencoe: The Free Press, 1957).
6. Conrad Arensberg, *The Irish Countryman* (New York: Macmillan, 1937).
7. In personal conversation.
8. "The Behavioral Sciences at Harvard," Report by a Committee of the Faculty, June, 1954, p. 293.
9. *Op. cit.*, "Identity and Totality," p. 57.

10. John P. Marquand, *The Late George Apley* (New York: Random House, 1936), Chap. 8, "The Interlude," pp. 84-92.

11. *Op. cit.*

12. M. Grodzins, "Making Un-Americans," *American Journal of Sociology,* LX (1955), 570-80; and *The Loyal and the Disloyal* (Chicago: The University of Chicago Press, 1956).

13. E. Hunter, *Brain-Washing in Red China: The Calculated Destruction of Men's Minds* (New York: Vanguard, 1951).

Since these pages were written I have seen materials closely paralleling Hunter's. Cf., "Staff Memorandum, Psychological Warfare Division," George Washington University; and "Wang Tsun Ming, Anti-Communist: An Autobiographical Account of Chinese Thought Reform." (I am indebted for this information to the late William C. Bradbury who was project director.) Cf. also Robert Lifton, "Thought Reform of Western Civilians in Chinese Communist Prisons," *Psychiatry,* XC (1956), 173-95.

14. *Op. cit.,* p. 32. The quotation is from a statement by a former student.

15. *Ibid.,* pp. 36-37.

16. *Ibid.,* p. 112.

17. This manuscript is not yet published.

18. Everett Hughes, "Cycles and Turning Points, The Significance of Initiation in Human Culture" (The National Council of the Episcopal Church, faculty paper).

19. Nelson Foote, "Concept and Method in the Study of Human Development," mimeographed manuscript of paper delivered at an Oklahoma conference in Social Psychology.

20. Harold Laski, *The American Presidency* (New York: Harper, 1940).

21. Erik H. Erikson, "Identity and Totality: Psychoanalytic Observations on the Problem of Youth," *Human Development Bulletin* (Fifth Annual Symposium, Committee on Human Development of the University of Chicago, 1954), pp. 51-55. See also Erikson's "The Problem of Identity," *American Journal of Psychoanalysis,* Vol. IV (1956).

22. *Ibid.*

23. Harry S. Sullivan, *The Interpersonal Theory of Psychiatry,* edited by H. Perry and M. Gamal (New York: Norton, 1953).

Chapter V

1. *Op. cit.*

2. W. Lloyd Warner, *A Black Civilization* (New York: Harper, 1937).

3. Margaret Mead, quoted in J. J. Honigman, *Culture and Personality* (New York: Harper, 1954), p. 346.

4. C. B. Stendler, "Sixty Years of Child Training Practices," *Pediatrics,* XXXVI (1950), pp. 122-34.

5. Karl Mannheim, "The Problem of Generations," in *The Sociology of Knowledge,* trans. by Paul Kecskemeti (New York: Oxford University Press, 1952), pp. 276-322.

6. *Ibid.,* p. 282.

7. *Ibid.,* p. 283.

8. O. Mannoni, *Psychologie de la Colonisation* (Paris: Editions du Seuil, 1950), Chap. 3, "La Succession des Générations et la Personalité," pp. 123-30.

9. *Op. cit.*, "The Problem of Identity," p. 57.

10. John Steinbeck, *The Wayward Bus* (New York: Viking, 1947), pp. 41-42.

11. Honoré de Balzac, *Old Goriot* (New York: Dutton, 1935).

12. Albert Camus, "Art in Revolt," *Partisan Review*, 1952, p. 275.

13. *Ibid.*

Chapter VI

1. Much of this section is taken from a paper titled "Concepts, Communication, Groups," published in M. Sherif and M. Wilson (eds.), *Social Relations at the Crossroads* (New York: Harper, 1953), pp. 99-105.

2. John Dewey, Experience and Nature (Chicago: Open Court, 1925).

3. M. Sherif, *An Outline of Social Psychology* (New York: Harper, 1948), p. 105.

4. M. Sherif and C. Sherif, *Groups in Harmony and Tension* (New York: Harper, 1953), p. 164.

5. Robert K. Merton and Alice S. Kitt, "Contributions to the Theory of Reference Group Behavior," in R. K. Merton and P. Lazarsfeld (eds.), *Continuities in Social Research* (Glencoe: The Free Press, 1950), pp. 86-87.

6. Georg Simmel, *The Web of Group-Affiliations*, trans. by Bendix, Reinhard (Glencoe: The Free Press, 1955), p. 139.

7. Lindesmith and Strauss, *op. cit.* (1949 ed.), p. 118.

8. J. Myers and L. Schaffer, "Social Stratifications and Psychiatric Practice: A Study of an Out-Patient Clinic," *American Sociological Review*, XIX (1954), p. 310.

9. Leonard Schatzman and Anselm Strauss, "Social Class and Modes of Communications," *American Journal of Sociology*, LX (1956), 329-38; and "Cross-Class Interviewing, An Analysis of Interaction and Communicative Styles," *Human Organization*, XIV (1956), 28-31.

10. Renée Fox, Ph.D. Thesis, Harvard University, Department of Social Relations.

11. *Mind, Self and Society*, pp. 157-58.

12. Unpublished manuscript, "Tourist Imagery and the Use of Cities."

13. J. Vandreyes, *Language* (New York: Alfred Knopf, 1925), p. 249.

14. Herbert Blumer, "Collective Behavior," in A. Lee (ed.), *New Outline of the Principles of Sociology* (New York: Barnes and Noble, 1946).

15. Tomatsu Shibutani, "Reference Groups as Perspectives," *American Journal of Sociology*, LX (1955), 565-67.

16. Osbert Sitwell, *Left Hand, Right Hand!* (Boston: Little and Brown, 1944).

17. Carleton J. Hayes, *Essays on Nationalism* (New York: Macmillan, 1926).

18. (New York: Harcourt Brace, 1949).

19. Everett C. Hughes, in conversation.

20. Stadtrat zu Nürnberg, *Lebendiges Nürnberg* (Nürnberg: Ulrich, 1953), p. 8.

21. Rebecca West, *Black Lamb and Grey Falcon* (New York: Viking, 1940), pp. 89-94.

22. Richard R. Wohl, "The Use of Sociological Concepts in Historical Research," a paper delivered at the national meetings of the American Sociological Society, 1956.

Chapter VII

1. John Gillin (ed.), *For a Science of Social Man* (New York: Macmillan, 1954), "Psychology and Sociology," pp. 67-101. The quotation may be found on p. 75.

2. Peter Blau, *The Dynamics of Bureaucracy* (Chicago: University of Chicago Press, 1955).